FISHLESS DAYS, ANGLING NIGHTS

SPARSE GREY HACKLE

FISHLESS DAYS, ANGLING NIGHTS

NICK LYONS BOOKS
WINCHESTER PRESS

Produced by
NICK LYONS BOOKS
212 Fifth Avenue
New York, NY 10010
Published and distributed by
WINCHESTER PRESS
New Century Publishers, Inc.
220 Old New Brunswick Road
Piscataway, NJ 08854
PRINTED IN THE UNITED STATES OF AMERICA
10 9 8 7 6 5 4 3 2 1

Library of Congress Cataloging in Publication Data

Hackle, Sparse Grey, 1892-
    Fishless days, angling nights.

    "A Nick Lyons book."
    1. Fishing—Anecdotes, facetiae, satire, etc.
    I. Title.
SH441.H13   1983   799.1'2   83-3551
ISBN 0-8329-0327-2

ACKNOWLEDGMENTS

A NUMBER OF THE ARTICLES IN THIS BOOK APPEARED EARLIER in *The Gordon Garland* and *The American Angler*; *The Sportsman* magazine; *Sports Illustrated* magazine; *Life* magazine's international edition; *The Anglers' Club Bulletin*; the *Flyfishers' Journal*; *Outdoor Life* magazine; and *Fishless Days*. They are reproduced here in whole or in part through the courtesy of Colonel Peter Vischer of Washington, D.C.; the Theodore Gordon Flyfishers, Inc.; Time-Life Inc.; Popular Science Publishing Co.; The Flyfishers' Club (London); and The Anglers' Club of New York.

A portion of "The First Camping Trip" originally appeared in somewhat different form and under the title "That Fall Guy" in the December 1955 issue of *Outdoor Life* magazine; copyright © 1955, Popular Science Publishing Co., Inc.

The author's warmest thanks are due to the following Crown Publishers, Inc., personnel:

Nick Lyons, for his astute editing, practical advice, aid, comfort, and limitless patience, which have made this book possible.

Miss Johanna Turnquist, for her perceptive, sophisticated, and expert copyreading.

CONTENTS

WOMAN IN WADERS

AT LEAST AS FAR BACK AS THE BEGINNING OF THIS CENTURY there were a few women who defied convention for the pleasure of fishing with the fly. Theodore Gordon, sage of the Neversink, had a feminine fishing companion and so did Frederick White, chronicler of the Beaverkill. But it was not until well after the First World War that women became a familiar sight on the stream. Apparently it was the dry fly that lured them there. It is significant that Gordon, father of the dry fly in America, and White, one of his early disciples, each taught his fair companion to cast upstream and float her fly over the broken water without drag. And the coming of the dry fly into general popularity coincides approximately with the coming of the woman angler.

The marvel is that it didn't happen sooner, for dry-fly fishing is more a woman's than a man's game. What are the requirements? Dexterity and good coordination, fast and well-controlled reflexes, a light and sensitive touch, keen eyesight, and close concentration. Any industrial personnel man will assure you that women are greatly superior to men in these respects. Too, they avoid the failings of men anglers. They never try to see how far or fancy they can cast, never daydream while fishing, and lack the mechanical bent which makes many a man more interested in his tackle than in his fishing.

Above all, these capable, experienced woman anglers have a hard, cold, relentless determination to kill and keep every fish they can get. There exists a group of woman anglers which undoubtedly represents the greatest concentration of feminine fly-fishing talent in the world. It would humiliate me to display my meager skill in their presence. Yet I can do one thing that they cannot; I can put back fish.

But skillful as they are, theirs is only the initial stage of feminine angling development. A few of them grow in spiritual stature until they are beyond all this female obsession with getting. And then they are no longer woman anglers. As my wife, who is indeed one of the elect, once firmly declared: "I am *not* a lady fly fisher; I am a fly fisherman."

Elevated to this hierarchy (*rank or order of angels*—Webster), woman becomes the Creator's masterwork made manifest, the true friend, the dear companion whose presence doubles the happiness of every stream hour and makes bright the evening when the anglers gather at the inn; the perfect sportsman who enjoys your good fortune more than you do and whose good fortune in turn exalts you.

Her utter devotion to the ideals of the sport produces the sublimation, the epitome, the archetype of the true angler.

It is this which makes my dear wife an angel of the first magnitude.

To Lady Beaverkill, Louise Brewster Miller, I therefore dedicate this book in memory of all our bright hours of angling together.

Prologue: ON NOT-CATCHING FISH

SOON AFTER I EMBRACED THE SPORT OF ANGLING I BECAME convinced that I should never be able to enjoy it if I had to rely on the cooperation of fish. Fortunately, I learned long ago that although fish do make a difference—*the* difference—in angling, catching them does not; so that he who is content to not-catch fish in the most skillful and refined manner, utilizing the best equipment and technique, will have his time and attention free for the accumulation of a thousand experiences, the memory of which will remain for his enjoyment long after any recollection of fish would have faded. From these memories, garnered over more than forty years of fishless days, I have set down some typical observations and cogitations. By and large the reporting is factual, but in a few instances I have claimed the right of readjusting the facts to which every angler is entitled.

FISHLESS DAYS,
ANGLING NIGHTS

WHO IS
SPARSE GREY HACKLE?

OVER THE LAST THIRTY-FIVE YEARS DISCUSSIONS OF VARIOUS aspects of angling have appeared under the pen name of Sparse Grey Hackle. And for approximately that length of time readers have demanded: "Who does Sparse Grey Hackle think he is?" I can answer that query.

It was on a June evening, back in the old days, that my friend Everett Garrison and I entered the barroom of The Antrim Lodge, where were gathered the innumerable fishermen who were spending the mayfly season at Roscoe, New York, trout-fishing capital of the Catskills. We found the low-ceiled basement already jammed with men in hobnailed shoes and waders who were either guarding their drinks with both hands or fighting their way through the crowd to the bar. A roar of conversation battled with the crash of the jukebox, and a blanket of tobacco smoke veiled the lights.

"This is hopeless. Let's go see Harry and Elsie and get a drink from them," I suggested. The reply came, not from

Garry but from a stranger beside me, a fat man with a red face and scanty white hair.

"The Darbees are fishing the East Branch and likely won't be home until midnight, but I'll be glad to give you a drink if you'll come upstairs to my room," he said.

He was a fisherman, by his tweeds and the wood-duck flank feather in his hatband; an old-timer if he knew Harry and Elsie Darbee, whom I call the best flytiers in the world, that well; and sober, although he had enough alcohol on his breath to take the varnish off a rod.

We accepted and went upstairs, where the stranger took a bottle from a whole case of Scotch and poured for us. The conversation turned to fishing, and finally Garry mentioned Old Bill, the twelve-pound brown trout that lived for years under the old covered bridge at Arena.

"A mere minnow," said our new-found friend. This nettled Garry, for of course a twelve-pound brown is an enormous fish.

"Yes?" he replied. "What's the biggest fish *you* ever caught?"

"I caught the biggest brown trout in the world. He weighed at least fifty pounds and he was well over five feet long," was the answer.

I curbed my natural reaction. After all, I was drinking the man's liquor.

"Didn't you weigh and measure him?" I asked when I could control my voice.

"He's still in the river," said the stranger. He paused to open a fresh bottle, poured himself a tumblerful, and began:

"I am a big-fish fisherman; anyone in Roscoe will tell you that Sparse Grey Hackle has never been known to take a trout under three pounds. As you probably know, everything about the time, place, and method of taking big trout is completely different from taking the ordinary stream fish. So the big-fish fishermen are a clannish, secretive group, and each one has his own distinctive method. My method is to think like a fish.

"About this time last year I got to wondering why no one catches trout in the Mountain Pool, so I put myself in the place of a fish and asked myself why I avoided such a fine pool. The answer was obvious: I was afraid. And what was there about that pool that I, a fish, need fear? Only one thing —a bigger fish. Big fish drive away the smaller ones.

"I reflected that no one had ever taken even a five-pound trout from the Mountain Pool, which could only mean that there must be a trout in there big enough to chase a five-pounder away. I resolved to get him.

"So next day at dawn I drove down to the Mountain Pool with all my tackle, my lunch of bread and cheese, and a case of Scotch. I put a couple of bottles in the seat of my waders so I wouldn't have to be running back to the car all the time. Then I rigged my big nine-foot rod and went to work.

"I fished with everything from dry flies to minnows without moving a fish, and then I tore my waders on the barbed-wire fence that Guy Bury built across the tail of the pool to keep his cows from straying. So I went back to the car and patched the waders, spilling a little pool of rubber cement in the process. While I was waiting for the patch to dry, a shower came up.

"As I sat huddled in my slicker I noticed the bugs on the ground; they were rolling in the rubber cement and then running around in the rain having a fine time. They were, you might say, wearing raincoats.

"This gave me an idea, one that would occur only to a man who thinks like a fish. I went back in the bushes and caught one of those huge moths, coated it with rubber cement, and stuck it onto my hook. Then I threw it in at the head of the pool and fed out line to let it float downstream naturally.

"The moth fluttered along the surface, rising a few inches and then dropping back. About halfway down the pool, there was a sucking sound and the moth disappeared in a swirl as big as a washtub!

"I struck as hard as I dared; there was a terrific convulsion in the water; I began to reel. . . . The next thing I knew I was in six feet of water and the line was reeled in right up to the leader knot. The fish was so big that I had reeled myself out to him instead of drawing him in to me! Gentlemen, I give you my word he was over five feet long and weighed fifty pounds if he weighed an ounce.

"In this emergency I began to think like a fish. What would I do if I were that big and I had a fisherman where he had me? I would chew the living hell out of him! Since I had no desire to be simultaneously the most famous and the deadest fisherman on the Beaverkill, I got out my knife and cut the line. But the fish got around between me and the shore, and I was having a terrible time with him when someone grabbed me by the collar and hoisted me ashore.

"It was Keegan, the state trooper who patrols Route 17 below Roscoe, where it runs beside the river. I was grateful to him for saving my life but exasperated because he had not even seen the big fish and intimated that I had been drinking. In fact, he threatened to run me in if I drank any more that day.

"When he left I went back to my car for my lunch and a couple more bottles. I dipped my bread in the whisky—I wasn't drinking the liquor; I was eating it, see?—and sat down to think like a fish. This was no ordinary fish, so it followed that he would not be interested in an ordinary lure. I put my mind to work to invent an extraordinary lure, and I did.

"I was starting on my second loaf of bread when I saw minnows breaking water in the shallows as if something were chasing them. So I soaked a slice of bread in whisky and let it float down the current. I figured that that old trout hadn't had a drink in years and would be eager for one. And I was right. As soon as he smelt the whisky he took up his feeding position, and when the bread came along he drifted up to it and—socko! I could hear his teeth clash. I took a bite of bread and poured whisky into my mouth on top of it, which is a handier way to eat Scotch, and then I soaked another slice and put it on my hook.

"The big trout hit it furiously but he just stole my bait. He stole the next three slices too. Then I noticed that he was weaving around in the current. He missed the next slice completely, floated downstream on his side, and began to swim in circles. And every little while he would open his mouth and emit a string of bubbles and a sound like 'Hup!'

"Then I sent him down a slice of bread with *two* hooks in it and when he gulped it I struck, hard. The rod bent down to the water. The reel began to screech and then to smoke, and in another instant the bearings burned out, the spool jammed, and the line broke. I thought I had lost the big fish but in a moment I saw him chasing minnows, upside down, with my line trailing behind him. I grabbed it and tied it to my wrist. It almost cost me my life.

"He started downstream like a torpedo, towing me behind him. He went through the barbed-wire fence like a bat out of hell, but I hit it with a bang that uprooted the posts. Tangled as I was in the wire I could not get to my feet so I started rolling to get ashore.

"The drunken trout lunged at me with his mouth open—and what teeth he had!—but just as he was about to bite me he said 'Hup!' so he hit me with his mouth closed. Even so, the point of his great undershot jaw cut a gash in my leg. He charged again, but again he hupped at the last moment, so all I got was another gash. Again and again he attacked but each time he would 'Hup!' and have to close his mouth. My legs were covered with gashes by the time Keegan hauled me ashore.

"Again he had failed to see the big fish; he said my cuts were from rolling in the barbed wire. I think he was going to pinch me, but just then an old Model A Ford went down the road.

" 'There's that damned deer poacher!' shouted Keegan and ran for his car.

"When I awoke it was dusk and I felt terrible, but I got out the Alka Seltzer and a couple more bottles of Scotch and began thinking like a fish. The big fellow must be feeling terrible too, I decided. So I rigged my big salmon rod, and when I heard him splashing in the shallows across the pool, I put a few Alka Seltzer tablets onto the hook and cast into the darkness. There was a splash and a haul on my line, and this time I struck with both hands and then began pulling and horsing as hard as I could to bring this big fish over to my side.

"You never heard such a commotion in your life! The fish didn't swim around much but sort of floundered, and yelled. I suppose you think a trout can't yell. Well, this one did, and swore too!

"I hauled that fish almost across the river by main strength. Then the line went slack. The fish came toward me, half out of water. Something hit me in the eye and on the nose, and began battering me, and all the while the fish was assaulting me it was shrieking and cursing.

"I went down in the water. When I scrambled up I was astounded to see Johnny Woodruff in front of me. Was I surprised, and was I mad!

" 'What are you doing in my pool?' I yelled. 'I just had the world's biggest trout on and you come along and make me lose him! Where are your stream manners? Get the hell out of here!'

"But Johnny was madder than I was. You know what he accused me of? He said he had been night-fishing on the other side when I cast across him, hooked him in the neck, and tried to drown him!

"He started for me again, and believe me, I was glad to see Keegan for the third time. I thought fast, this time not like a fish but like a state trooper. I hauled out my remaining bottle.

" 'You need a drink after chasing that poacher,' I said.

" 'I been after him all summer; he's selling deer,' said Keegan, mentioning the worst sin in the Catskills. 'I got the goods on him at last. I slapped the cuffs on him and turned him over to Roy Steenrod (the game protector at that time) to take down to Liberty.' And with that he poured down a drink big enough to keep his radiator from freezing all winter.

" 'If you're wounded you had better guard against infection,' I advised Johnny. He took the bottle and sterilized his whole interior.

" 'And in these wet clothes I must take precautions against

pneumonia,' I concluded, and took all the precautions there were left in the bottle.

"While we were walking back to the car for another bottle I told them about the fifty-pound trout, but they only laughed. They wouldn't believe me! They wouldn't be—"

The speaker's voice had been dropping lower and lower, and now it stopped. A snore sounded.

Garry and I looked at each other, and tiptoed away.

* * *

The foregoing narrative is unreliable as to details, names, and places, and contains some misleading although technically correct statements—Sparse Grey Hackle never took a trout *over* three pounds, either! But it faithfully portrays the faulty observation and fallacious reasoning from unjustified assumptions to unwarranted conclusions that characterize the ordinary fisherman and cause him to "think like a fish"; *a fish does not think at all!*

In other words, Sparse Grey Hackle is just an ordinary angler, even as you and I.

THE YOUNG
CONSERVATIONIST

WHEN JOHN MILLER CAME TO WETHERSFIELD, CONNECTICUT, from Sussex, England, he was a farmer, and farmers his descendants remained right through nine generations into the early manhood of my father and his brother. True, my grampa took his young family to the Pennsylvania oil fields to make his fortune barging oil in barrels on Oil Creek; my father was born in a lease shack on the Tarr Farm, site of the world's first gusher. But the pipeline came and Grampa went broke; thereafter he was, variously, a drill-rig engineer, a coastwise trader in vegetables, a horsecar conductor, a Sing Sing prison guard, a customhouse clerk, a door-to-door salesman of patent oil lamps and, later, of life insurance, and a storekeeper in Tarrytown, New York.

But first, last, and in between he was a farmer, and managed or operated dairy farms from Lewes, Delaware, to Ballston Spa, New York, including two on Staten Island, even then a part of the city of New York. When he died at the age of eighty-three on a tiny subsistence farm in Orangeburg,

New York, he still had a plow horse, a Jersey cow, and one milk customer.

In my boyhood we spent our summers on Grampa's farm and in his late years it was my job to service that one customer. So each day, after an early supper, as soon as Grampa came in from milking, I'd set off with my two-quart pail, trudging up the Sparkill road in the afterglow of a summer sunset.

There are no roads like that one any more. It was a dim dirt lane that meandered through old meadows growing up to brush and trees, almost a tunnel under the great overhanging branches where the air was sweet with fresh-cut hay, spicy with weeds, and perfumed by the sun-warmed fruit of abandoned orchards. Each clump of woods provided a zone of cool air fragrant of cedar, and each marshy spot yielded the dank, earthy smell of mosses. It was so quiet, so still; nothing moved in that breathless evening hour and even my footsteps were silent in the dust of the road, fine and soft as talcum, a grateful cushion for a little boy's bare feet.

Once emptied, the pail had to be rinsed in a tiny spring brook that ran beside the road a ways. It flowed less than a kitchen faucet would, and it must have been fresh out of the ground for it was so cold my bare feet could not stand it. But it had the mystery of all running water, it provided crisp peppery watercress which no little boy could resist, and best of all, it was populous with frogs.

Boys and frogs have gone together ever since there were boys and frogs, and I entered joyfully into my heritage. Instinct taught me that a frog could be trapped in a hurled lump of mud, made to spring into an open hand or even a milk pail by touching his opposite end, or just by pouncing on him. So each evening I put a little water in my milk pail and then added half a pail of frogs. For I had a mission.

Across the road from our farmhouse was a marshy meadow and beyond it curved a little brook, a feeder of Sparkill Creek. It was a gentle, purling, cool, clear brook that was my favorite playground; I caught my first speckled trout in it. But there was one thing about it that puzzled me. There weren't any frogs in it; at least, none that I ever saw or heard. It seemed to me that when we sat out on the porch evenings under the magnolias, we were entitled to have the night noises of birds, katydids, and crickets accented and dramatized by the juggurums of a goodly frog population. Obviously, this was an oversight of Nature, and Alfred Miller was just the boy to show Nature how things should be done. So for some weeks I paused at one end of my milk run to load frogs and at the other end to liberate them. Then one evening I forgot to liberate them.

Here is where Gramma came into the story. Gramma was six feet tall, a Hempstead of Saxon bone and bulk, and she lived for battle; if no battle was handy, it was her delight to start one. She had a short-fuse temper and a rampaging sense of humor, as well as a great mop of blonde hair turned sort of white and a pretty good soprano voice—and lots of it. She was the ramrod, the driver that had really got the family through the terrible starving times of the seventies and eighties. She was thirteen years younger than Grampa and, as I remember it, she was always bossing him around and giving him a hard time. But six months after he died, she just sat down in her big old rocking chair and died of "heart trouble." But it wasn't heart failure; it was heartbreak.

In summertime we used an old board shack beside the well

for a summer kitchen because it was handier to the water supply, and cooler. It had a dirt floor, an old table and chairs, a kerosene cooking stove, and a wooden sink with a pail of well water and a tin dipper beside it. This night Gramma was sitting on a high stool washing the supper dishes and belting out "The Son of Man Goes Forth to War" like a captain leading a charge. Without missing a note she took the lid off the milk pail and abstractedly poured a cascade of indignant batrachians into the dishpan.

Gramma weighed three hundred pounds and she was lame besides, but she unloaded off that stool and sashayed out the door like a schoolgirl while hitting the highest, loudest note I ever heard her emit. She came back instantly, mad enough to chew nails. Any little boy who did that to his loving Gramma deserved, she opined, A Good Whipping; and she strongly implied that she was ready, willing, and able to do the job right then. As Gramma had raised four kids with a short-handled buggy whip, the situation looked a bit critical. But my mother, who was wiping the dishes, came to my rescue. My mother was meek and mild, but she was tougher than boiled rawhide; and she and Gramma didn't like each other very well anyway. She allowed softly that nobody—*nobody*— was going to whip her little Alfred. This confrontation provided the diversion I needed to retrieve my livestock and head for the marsh. I didn't return until Gramma had departed the shack.

The curious part of this adventure is that despite my exertions and the risking of my backside in the cause of conservation, I never afterward heard so much as a single croak from our stretch of the brook. The ungrateful little beggars must have taken off for other parts as soon as they were freed.

THE MAGIC CARPET

URBAN THOUGH I AM BY BIRTH AND BREEDING, I HAVE BEEN obsessed from my earliest boyhood with the idea of camping out. I never had opportunities to do so as a little boy, but I had something even better—a bureau drawer full of the catalogs of sporting goods, fishing tackle, firearms, and camping equipment dealers. What trips I took on the magic carpet of their pages! How often I stowed my Preston Mess Kit, my Marble waterproof matchbox, my Rainbow reel and Saline enameled line in my Nessmuk packsack, put them, with my Bristol rod, Colt's .45 six-shooter and Winchester .30-30 carbine, in my King folding canvas boat, and rowed away with my Lyman bow-facing oars.

Those were the best trips I ever took. I caught more fish and shot more game and saw more wild and wonderful woods and waters on them than on any trips I ever really took, and it never rained. I am still grateful to the fine old New York sporting goods houses, which in those days of cheap printing did not hesitate to bestow free on even a little boy a catalog as large as many present-day magazines and crammed with the most delectable prose and alluring pictures that ever enabled a prisoner to escape on the wings of fancy.

There was a richness and stimulation in those catalogs that made prosaic objects glow with splendor and seem infinitely desirable. Take so simple a thing as a knife—Marble's Hunting Knife. "Tang and blade forged in one piece, of high carbon tool steel." It was a great disappointment to me to learn years later that the difference between high-carbon and low-carbon steel is only a small fraction of 1 percent, and that tool steel is not the royalty of the ferrous metal kingdom but something the apprentice boys turn out while the real men are making nickel-chromium-moly, air-hardening high-speed, and other aristocratic alloys.

"Bleeding grooves on either side of the blade"—Wow!— "and oval bone-chopping edge on back of point." Anyone who couldn't see himself using that knife to dress out a deer which he had just shot with that rifle leaning against the pine, while the Indian guide . . . Anyone who couldn't see that just didn't have blood enough to run down a groove!

"The handle is formed of alternate washers of red and black hard fiber, brass and leather driven onto the tang and secured with a buckhorn screw tip, making a handle which will not slip even when covered with blood or grease."

What a picture! You are at grips with a grizzly bear. You snatch out your trusty Marble's Hunting Knife and plunge it into his throat. Blood spurts out and covers the handle, but does it slip? No! The alternate washers of red and black hard fiber, brass and leather "afford a firm, secure hold" and you do not even cut your hand, for "a neat cross-hilt prevents the hand from slipping down onto the blade when sticking a carcass." So you continue whittling into the grizzly until he falls over. Golly, who wouldn't pay $3.25 for such a magical knife!

Not all the catalog writing was so pure in heart; some of it was downright deceptive in those pre-Federal Trade Commission days. And the king of all these artists in deception, a con man who deceived the sportsmen of the nation for a generation, was the inventor of the African Steel Vine fishing rod.

Forty or fifty years ago Tonkin cane was just coming in as a rod-making material, difficult and expensive to get, and hard to work; the makers of the cheap machine-made rods that composed the bulk of the industry's output stuck to the easier-handled, cheaper, and more readily available Calcutta cane, with which they were familiar. The defect of Calcutta is that it has no backbone and produces soft, whippy rods. It remained for some unsung genius of roguery to further weaken and soften these weepers by cutting the corners off their hexagonal construction and turning them in a lathe until they were as round as a lead pencil. And then he christened the material African Steel Vine.

The catalog copywriters let their imagination expand without stint in extolling the marvelous qualities of this vine, a material about which none of them actually knew anything for the excellent reason that it did not exist. It was a conspiracy of deceit that succeeded so completely that I will wager few who remember the African Steel Vine rod at all have any idea yet what it was made of. Even the great Theodore Gordon fell for the hoax. Lacking mechanical aptitude and apparently at times a careless reader, he confused Steel Vine with the growth more familiar to him and called it "grapevine," but there is no doubt that it was the masquerading material that he referred to twice under that name in his writings.

Gordon mentioned "grapevine cane" in the *Fishing Gazette* in January 1907, to wonder what it was, and again in the same publication on July 6, 1907, when he wrote:

"Recently I saw a very pretty light rod of good action which had been made from the so-called grapevine cane. First I was told that the material was of African origin, again that it came from South America, that it grew to be of large size, and for fifty or sixty feet of the same diameter.

"The grain is perfectly straight and the sections for a hexagonal rod are easily split out or cut with a machine. In the finished rod the wood strongly resembles cane of light color, or from which the markings and cuticle have been planed away. The rod was beautifully finished in the best style and the price was but twelve dollars. . . .

"There may be possibilities in this wood, but I confess that this is the only good rod composed of it that I thought well of or liked at all."

It was through the magic carpet that I became interested in the greatest outdoors writer of them all, who did more than any other man, in my estimation, to shape the American concept of camping out. The recurrence of the name Nessmuk in connection with various articles of equipment always piqued my curiosity, but it was years before I learned that it was the pen name of George Washington Sears, high priest of the cult of "going to the North Woods," that swept to a nearly hysterical popularity during the period of his writings. For although he contributed voluminously to *Forest and Stream* magazine for some thirty years, his only book save for a small collection of his verses was *Woodcraft,* a little thin volume so fascinating that I have read two copies of it literally to pieces—so fascinating that it has stayed in print for nearly fifty years.

Nessmuk was the originator and prophet of the "go light" movement that had for its gospel the idea of camping with as little equipment as possible. He went into the woods with only a couple of tin dishes, a small muslin shelter, a blanket bag, and a little pocket ax. He induced Rushton, a Canton, New York, canoemaker, to build for him a series of light craft culminating in the ten-pound *Sairy Gamp,* which hangs now in The Adirondack Museum on loan from the Smithsonian Institution, its owner. He boasted that his whole outfit, including canoe, fishing rod, and a week's food, weighed but twenty-six pounds; and he lashed with ridicule anyone who carried heavy equipment or even wore heavy clothing in the woods. What he never added was that he himself was a little man weighing 105 pounds and so had a great advantage over anyone heavier.

Nessmuk was an interesting and complex personality about whom I wish I knew more. He was a snappy and flamboyant character who lived on controversy and did not fear the limelight. He loved nothing better than to paddle at sunset up to the dock of some Adirondack resort hotel and become the center of a respectfully admiring throng of bored guests who had been expecting him all afternoon. In the eighties he made several well-advertised trips through the resort area of the North Woods, but he spent little time, if any at all, under canvas; he was always too much in demand in the bar, on the porch, or in the guide camp to which the boarders flocked nightly for atmosphere.

There is a queer contradiction in Nessmuk's personality

which manifests itself in the things he wrote and did not write. For one thing, there is a curious streak of saltwater running through his writings; he loves to speak of "two bells in the morning watch" (he apparently meant the midwatch) and rousing the sleepers with "Starbowlins ahoy!" Yet aside from a passenger trip to Brazil in later life, his only blue-water experience came when he shipped on a whaler and became so violently and incurably seasick that he was put ashore at the Azores to save his life, and came home as a passenger.

On the other hand, at the outbreak of the Civil War, Nessmuk was for several months a member of a very valorous, proud, and famous Pennsylvania regiment, the Pennsylvania Bucktails, being discharged in consequence of a foot or ankle injury. This made him at least as much of a soldier as he was a sailor. Furthermore, the years after the Civil War during which he did most of his writing were deeply imbued with a military spirit that manifested itself in such things as the Baptist Boys Brigades and other Sunday school military organizations, uniformed and drilled fraternal orders, and the curious camping-out custom of each man having his own grub box, coffeepot, and frying pan, and preparing his own meal at a common cooking fire. Yet I do not recall a single military turn of phrase or expression in Nessmuk's writings. I wish I knew what experience so deeply disaffected a man who seems, from here, to have been cut out for a soldier.

Foibles aside, let us give Nessmuk his due. He was a master woodsman, hunter (professional, at one time), and canoeman who engaged actively in these pursuits from the time he was a little boy until he was past seventy, winter and summer, fair weather and foul, taking many chances and the luck as it came even though he suffered from tuberculosis during most of his life and eventually died of it. Above all, he was a writer with a magic pen on which he played like the Pied Piper's flute to lure the grown-up children of the budding industrial age away from their desks and workbenches into the make-believe of the sylvan glades.

Dig up a copy of *Woodcraft*—they can still be had cheap enough—and if you want something to carry you from your easy chair to the deep woods, read Nessmuk's description of his long journey alone through the trackless Michigan forest and, in his chapter "Shelters," his description of a hunter lost in the November woods spending the night in an improvised "Indian camp." He can fascinate you, that man. No wonder Horace Kephart dedicated his monumental *Camping and Woodcraft* to Nessmuk, "the master of them all."

THE FIRST
CAMPING TRIP

A MAN'S FIRST TRY AT ANYTHING, FROM FLYING AN AIRPLANE to just going camping, is many things but above all, educational. He learns more—the things that aren't in the books—that first time than a hundred repetitions will teach him.

Take, for instance, the time my boy Bill and his pal "Lightning" Lighthall, each then about twelve or thirteen years old, decided that it would be a diverting caper to camp overnight on the town bathing beach of our small Connecticut community. The beach was crowded all day (this was in August) but completely deserted at night; the sand was soft and warm so no bedding would be needed; and they could have a few swims in the late evening and early morning with the beach all to themselves.

They had never heard of the go-light craze, but believe me, they could have given old Nessmuk and his superlight outfit cards and spades, for their entire equipment consisted of one can of beans and one fork. No shelter; no can opener—Bill never amplified his brief statement that they "opened it with a pointed rock"; and they saved the weight of an extra fork by taking turns with the one they had. Besides khaki pants, shirts, and sneakers, they had their bathing trunks and, at my wife's insistence, a light jacket apiece; and Lightning wore a hard straw hat over his white-blond crew-cut thatch while Bill went bareheaded.

The boys came home afoot early next morning instead of waiting for the prearranged car pickup, and no amount of questioning could elicit any details of their experiences. They ate inconceivable numbers of my wife's pancakes and then went up to Bill's room and closed the door.

After three hours of utter silence in that quarter my wife opened the door a crack and peeked. Fully dressed, the boys were flaked out crosswise on Bill's bed, Lightning still wearing his stiff straw hat. They came down in midafternoon, ate another enormous meal, and disappeared still enveloped in dignified silence.

I didn't need to ask because when I was seventeen and my cousin Frank sixteen, we went through the same thing. Canoeing around in the lower end of the Hutchinson River one day we spotted a rocky outcrop called Goose Island; it had a sort of rock step halfway up one side, perfectly flat and level. We would camp there! So we went home—Frank lived nearby —for permission and food. This consisted of sandwiches, but Frank insisted on real camping so he made a cooking pot by putting a wire bail on a tin can, and brought along a big ear of corn to cook.

We hauled the canoe up ten or twelve feet onto the rock ledge and turned it on its side at the outer edge for shelter.

Against the rock wall we built our fire. (We were camping, weren't we? Campers always have fires; it says so in the books.) For a mattress we had the carpet from the bottom of the canoe—remember, the rock was perfectly smooth—and for bedding we had my raincoat—remember, it was hot August weather.

We ate the sandwiches, boiled the corn one end at a time and each ate his half; darn good even without salt or butter. Then, although it was still daylight, we went to bed as all novice campers insist on doing. Frank was nearest the fire and it was too hot so he got up and put it out, but in a few hours we bitterly regretted the lack of it because of course it turned as cold as the Arctic. The perfectly smooth rock mysteriously started to grow bumps, too, which kept us shifting and squirming until finally we got up; after a while lay down again; and for the rest of the night got up and lay down like a pair of jumping jacks. Frank had to go to work so we broke camp early, which was no hardship at all. We went home for a big breakfast and a change of clothes, and then Frank departed gravy-eyed for the trolley and I turned in on his bed for a few hours' sleep. Then I got more sandwiches and all the bedding my aunt could spare and took the whole load back to Goose Island. I paddled into the shallows where high salt grass grew in endless vistas and went to work with my jackknife cutting one canoeload after another and laying them up neatly on the rock shelf until I had a bed six feet square and darn close to three feet thick. It took all afternoon, but when I had spread a lot of quilts and blankets over it it was fit for two kings.

I picked up Frank at the boat landing after work, and we paddled through the late afternoon stillness with the whole green-banked river to ourselves, hauled up the canoe and ate our sandwiches, sat by our fire until *nine* o'clock, and then turned in. Neither of us moved or opened an eye until the morning sun started broiling us.

First camping trips don't usually produce much actual trouble, but a friend of mine found some his first time out. Ned went far into the woods in the Schroon Lake area, alone except for his dog, for his initiation. He had taken counsel and is a smart fellow besides, and he was well-found; but the things that aren't in the book tripped him.

First, he got lost in a maze of old tote roads that did not conform to the Geological Survey maps; he didn't know that all too many of those old trails were sketched in freehand (or worse) by impatient surveyors. He was carrying a big Duluth packsack with a head-strap, or tumpline, on it and of course the straps pressed tightly against the sides of his head. This put a pressure on his rimless glasses that they had not been built to withstand, so the next thing was that they broke in two at the nosepiece. As he had no extra pair with him *(and don't ever let this happen to you!)* he had to navigate thereafter by holding one lens to each eye with his hands; and if you think that makes for easy woods travel, try it.

Then his dog caught a porcupine.

Well, a good man, which Ned was and is, rises to emergencies. He managed somehow to make a camp, jury-rig his glasses with adhesive tape and a straight twig, and then get the worst of the quills out of his dog; and in the morning found his way back to civilization and a veterinarian.

By contrast, my old schoolmate Ed Curtiss hit the jackpot on his first trip. Ed used to vacation at a "camp" on Fourth

Lake—sleep in tents, on cots, and eat in a wooden dining hall. Standard procedure was to sleep and swim all day, and dance and drink bootleg Canadian ale (those were Prohibition times) all night. One day someone got to talking about real camping, and first thing you know a mass "sleep-out" was ready for the trail early one morning. These were all greenhorns, and you can imagine that the "packs" they made up were fearful and wonderful—everything from the old Spanish war doughnut blanket-roll over one shoulder to the good old-fashioned suitcase. But they had one thing in common: everyone knew firsthand that the nights got cold up there, so all the packs were good and big—plenty of bedding.

No friend of unnecessary labor, Ed looked at these burdens with a calculating eye and hit on a plan. When he showed up at the start, all he had was a small, neatly tied package under one arm. "All a good camper needs is a heavy sweater and a toothbrush," he declared when they exclaimed in astonishment, and stubbornly withstood a storm of kidding.

They started off. The woods were hot and close, the trail rough and the campers soft, so the big clumsy packs soon had everyone stumbling and sweating. As they wearied their good nature vanished, and their kidding turned to indignation and threats as they saw Ed skipping along so lightly with his little parcel.

"You'll be sorry!" they stormed when he jeered at them. "It will be cold tonight. Don't come around begging for blankets you didn't help carry. You're going to freeze and we're going to laugh at you."

They halted in an open glade, hacked down a dead tree, built their bonfire, scorched their hot dogs, and sat around singing while it got colder than Greenland's icy mountains.

Then they made up their nice warm beds, laughing hilariously at Ed who sat quietly by the fire until everyone had turned in. Then he picked out the chap with the biggest, softest, thickest, warmest bed and approached him.

"How about letting me share your bed?" he asked. The reply was prompt, emphatic, profane, and negative.

"I have a bottle of whisky," said Ed softly. The man stared at him incredulously, then swept back the blankets with a swift gesture.

"Get in here quick before anyone sees it," he urged.

And finally, there were the six boys, twelve or thirteen years old, who went camping along the upper Susquehanna when the glass mill in Pittston, Pennsylvania, in which several of them worked, shut down. In a one-room wooden cabin by the river, I was camping for fifteen days between two tours of duty with the National Guard at Tobyhanna. It had rained hard every day for five days (and, parenthetically, it did the same thing for the next ten) . During a letup I went down the road to get water from a spring and discovered that these boys had made camp in a narrow clearing beside the road.

I never saw anything like it. They had a big, heavy wall tent, about ten by fifteen feet, with huge wooden poles, ridge, and pins; wooden soapboxes full of canned goods—mostly corn, tomatoes, and fruit; a big china soup tureen, china soup plates and dinner plates, cups and saucers; enough straw for bedding to cover the floor of the tent about one straw deep; one piece of carpet to lie on and one quilt to cover them; no ax; a gallon of kerosene in a glass jug and a little old-fashioned two-wick oil stove just like what my grandmother used to heat a curling iron—it gave about as much heat as a fair-sized oil lamp, but they intended to cook for six on it.

They had pitched right at the foot of a precipitous slope, down which, that very morning, I had seen a torrent of rain-water cascading; and they were out in the road happily play-ing ball with no heed to the black, threatening clouds over-head.

"Boys," I counseled, "you'd better ditch around that tent good and deep. Go to that shack up the road, tell them I sent you, and borrow a pick and shovel." (I had made friends with a neighbor.)

"Yes, sir," they said courteously—they were awfully nice boys—and went on playing catch. An hour later I went back to check up. No ditch, ball game still going on. I recognized the uselessness of trying to tell a boy anything.

"Look, fellows," I told them. "If it gets too tough, come on up to my cabin around the bend."

"Yes, sir. We'll be all right. But thank you anyway, sir."

I stacked more dry firewood on the roofed porch of my shack, made all snug, and sat down on the old sofa I had dragged out there to sleep on. I had not long to wait. With a crash and a flash the sky split apart and Niagara Falls de-scended; I never saw it rain harder. I thought of the boys and what they must be getting and finally was just reaching for my raincoat to go down after them when a safari came around the bend of the road.

Six drowned rats—six boys as wet as if they had forded the river hat-deep—each bearing on his head a wooden soap-box heaped with impedimenta, filed into the cabin and stacked their stuff neatly. I opened the big doors (the cabin was really a "portable garage" with a little porch added) and got a big fire going, and after a while they dried out fairly well. Apparently they didn't mind being wet, anyway.

The rain continued and soon it was plain that they would have to spend the night with me, so they started the preparation of their first meal. They ripped open several cans of corn, dumped them into a saucepan, added not less than half a pound of butter, and fired up the oil stove, which produced volumes of soot and smoke without making any apparent impression on the temperature of the corn. But eventually the butter melted and with that dinner was served. The corn was ladled into stone-cold plates, the butter congealing instantly in a solid layer, bread was cut and buttered, and then the nauseating mess was shovelled down with real gusto; and the meal concluded with that standby of boyhood, bread and butter with a thick layer of sugar.

I knew they were in for a bad night and tried to keep them up long enough so that at least they would be tired when they went to bed; but like all novices they were hell-bent to turn in as soon as they were through eating. So dirty dishes and pots were shoved into a corner, the carpet was spread on the cement floor, and I retired to my couch on the porch.

Fully dressed even to caps and shoes, six boys sat down side by side on the carpet filling it from edge to edge. Twelve hands gripped the upper edge of the one quilt. Then, at the word, six boys lay down on their backs and drew the quilt up to their chins. It just covered them, with no turn-under at sides or bottom.

Each boy said, "Good night, Mr. Miller," courteously— they were really well brought-up, those boys. Each boy said "Good night" to each of the other five boys and received a "Good night" in return. A moment of silence ensued. Then:

"Hey, keep quiet."

"Ouch, get off me."

"Stop wiggling."

"Hey, don't do that. Now see what you went and did. We're all uncovered. Sit up, everybody."

They sat up and repeated the drill. They repeated the good nights in full detail. Again silence reigned briefly and then:

"Hey, cut it out. . . ."

You can repeat this often enough to fill several hours; then exhaustion and youth came to their rescue. When I finally took a peek at them they were wound together like a pail of eels, but all sound asleep.

They broke out at the first gray of dawn, repacked their traps, and tiptoed silently away—a boy's idea of silence, that is, broken by sibilant whispers, clumping feet, and rattling crockery. I had just finished shaving, cooking a good breakfast, and cleaning up when the heavens split once more. And after a while here came the safari again.

"Look, fellows, this is going to keep up for days," I told them. "When it lets up, go down and get your tent and store it under the porch, and figure on staying here until the weather changes."

Our captain had sent us off to the artillery school equipped as for war, with a long old-issue overcoat, a bedsack, six blankets, and who knows what-all. I can't remember the details now, but somehow I made shift to provide everybody with some sort of bed and bedding and organize the cooking so that nobody starved to death. I jacked the boys up hard on the dirty dishes—I'm hell on a clean camp—and as soon as they got the idea they turned to with all the willingness and good spirit in the world.

They were such nice boys; I had an awful lot of fun with them. One was named Patsy and was a trumpeter in his Boy Scout troop, and wrote to me when I was in France in the First World War and sent me his picture. If this should come to his eye or that of any of the other boys, I'd like to hear from them. [I never did.]

We took walks together and climbed up and down the mountain, and they watched me while I tried to fish a little. We made big fires and sat by them and told stories, and—I don't know, just sort of fooled around and chewed the rag. You can't remember what made good times under such circumstances; it seems trivial and flat in the telling. But we all had a good time, and I was grateful to them for such good company. I was sorry indeed when their week was up and they went home as they had come, by hitching rides on a wagon.

*   *   *

As I have indicated, the firstfruits of camping is experience, and experience breeds advice. There is never much demand for this commodity however great its excellence, but sometimes a man of goodwill is tempted to try and help his fellow man by raising the voice of experience. It has long been plain to me that most of the problems, trials, and vexations of camping relate back to mere weight. So once I philosophized about weight as follows:

The story is that one day long ago an apple fell off a tree upon the skull of Sir Isaac Newton, who forthwith discovered the principle of gravitation. Ever since, outdoorsmen have had to reckon with gravity.

If you're a beginner at camping, take my advice and learn

to live with "G," as aviators call this gremlin. It can make you a lot of trouble.

Take water, now. It's handy stuff in small lots for washing dishes, in larger lots for fishing, and in wholesale quantities for boating and swimming. Drops of water combined with "G" are called rain, and because there's so little you can do about it, rain is bad news on a camping trip.

When rain hits, "G" makes it run downhill into the little hollow in which you've pitched your tent. Then you're likely to sleep wet. Camping books say you can prevent this disaster by digging a nice deep ditch all around your tent, sloping the bottom so that the water will drain off instead of flooding the ditch. But this idea has several important things the matter with it. Sometimes it takes a pretty good civil engineer to get all that sloping and slanting done right.

When I was in East Texas with the Mexican Border Patrol, we got flooded out of our big pyramidal tents every time we had a rainstorm because our ditches were too small and sloped all ways. We never were able to keep dry until we dug ditches a foot wide and a foot deep, and linked them in an elaborate system of waterways which we pitched the right way by using the "battery commander's telescope" (an angle-measuring instrument) as a surveyor's level.

You may be able to ditch a tent without engineering instruments so that the water will flow away from it instead of under it. It's possible; but just how do you ditch a tent without a shovel? And how can you carry a shovel on a backpacking trip when you even have to take the pits out of the prunes beforehand to save weight?

All right, you have a shovel that doesn't weigh anything! But have you ever tried to dig a ditch, or anything else, in the woods? Well, the forest floor contains more roots than dirt. I won't say you can't dig through it, but I'd rather be watching than helping when you try.

Personally, I don't do much about ditching unless I happen to have a lot of root-grubbing tools handy. Usually I just try to camp on loose, sandy soil and then pray that it won't rain too hard. This defeats "G" most of the time.

However, I'll pitch in a hollow any time if that's the only way to get on level ground. It rains only part of the time, but "G" never stops. You'll notice that if you try sleeping on a surface that has the least bit of slant. A pitch too slight for your eye to detect will keep you rolling, or, worse, trying not to roll, all night long. If you *have* to sleep on a slant have your head, not your feet, highest; and never try to sleep *across* a slant.

There are various outdoors matters on which it's best to try to compromise with "G." The smallest and lightest tent, for instance, is not necessarily the best. I once made myself a one-man tent that fitted me like a nightgown. There was no room for my outfit or for a little dry wood for the morning fire. In rain it leaked every time I touched it, despite its waterproofing. It got wet inside from my breath and by morning it stank. A tent with a little extra room is worth the little extra weight.

One insidious way in which "G" gets in its work in tents concerns pants. Pants are made to stand up in, and they depend on "G" to make what you put in the pockets stay put. When you lie down, "G" will coax little objects like pipes and jackknives out of your pocket and sneak them under the edge of the tent so you can never find them again. The only sure defense against this is a sewed-in ground cloth.

Such a ground cloth has another important use. Without it a tent is just a big piece of cloth that you can pull into any shape you please, all of them wrong except one. But if it has a sewed-in ground cloth it will have one definite shape, and once you've pegged down the floor, each pole and stake can go in only one place, the right one. Very nice when you're pitching in the rain.

Another thing worth the extra weight is an air mattress. People will tell you to smooth off the ground and make a bed of balsam boughs on it. I say, leave the lumps and throw an air mattress over them. Even if you can find evergreens and are allowed to cut them, which is far from certain nowadays, you can spend a whole afternoon making a browse bed that you won't like very well that night. I'll leave food home, if necessary, to make room for an air mattress.

You can save a little "G" trouble by using a sleeping bag instead of blankets, but if you intend to keep a fire going or have any other reason for getting up during the night, you'll be happier with a bag that's easy to get in and out of. Mummy bags that have to be crawled into from the top are not in that class. You might also note that a few people are temperamentally unsuited to sleeping in bags. My most hilarious camping memory is of a partner who dreamed a bull was chasing him and tried to run away inside a crackling canvas sleeping bag. It sounded like two skeletons wrestling on a tin roof.

Still another place where old Sir Isaac's "G" shows up strong is around the cooking fire. Though the books give advice about broiling, roasting, and boiling camp food instead of frying it, you'll quickly find that the frying pan is the camp's basic weapon. But, oh, my aching back, what frying pans they are!

For some reason, women have a bad habit of hammering or warping a big bulge into the bottom of every frying pan they get hold of. So if you're using a utensil that's a fugitive from a kitchen, it will be sure to rock drunkenly and stand every way but level when you put it on the fire. If it's the extra-light type of small pan favored by many campers and the handle proves to be heavier than the pan, you'll be in a terrible fix.

What all this leads to is that when the pan tilts off the exact level, "G" will make the grease flow onto one side and off the other. Then the grease on the bare side will start to burn. Since like all new campers you're using "a thick bed of hot coals," your pan will start to burn immediately and ruin your bacon and eggs.

Build your cooking fire between two parallel logs or piles of stones that are longer than the fire. Put your frying pan across the logs or stone-piles but alongside the fire, not over it. Be positive that the pan bottom is well supported on a true level. Then with a stout stick rake coals out of the fire and under your pan. Keep replacing them as they burn to ashes. This gives you heat you can control, protection against scorched knuckles, and no burned grease.

"G" will also remind you that modern man is an upright animal who's uncomfortable crouching by a fire. You'll yearn for a table you can stand up to. I've read that you can make one, or anything else from a pothook to a two-story bungalow, out of forked sticks. But have you ever tried to drive a green forked stick into the ground? It springs instead of penetrating, and when you hit it harder it splits. Maybe you can push it in, but drive it? It splits, friend; it splits most every time.

One place where "G" really comes into its own is in connection with the pack. The most important thing about it is the back and shoulders that carry it. Get in shape and any pack big and sturdy enough to hold your stuff will do your job. How you wear it is another matter. There's a strong tendency among beginners to let out the shoulder straps until the pack rests on what I might call the roof of the wearer's back porch. Sir Isaac Newton says you shouldn't do that. At every step you'll be using good muscle to move that heavy load not forward but upward, and it will soon wear you out. Hitch your pack so high that you won't lift or roll it at every step.

In connection with packing, tumplines—carrying straps that loop across the forehead—offer some unsolved problems. You can't wear a head-strap over a hat without ruining the hat and being uncomfortable besides; if you try it bareheaded the sun's in your eyes, black flies chew on your scalp, and brush snags your hair. I don't think much of tumplines; but they have a unique virtue. If you are on footing where you are likely to slip and fall, one short motion of your head will throw off the tumpline and of course the whole pack. A man hits the ground much faster, and harder, with a pack than without one; be careful about falls.

One way in which campers, particularly new ones, try to mitigate the evils of "G" is to use "combination" equipment to save weight. Combinations are apt to be fairly unsatisfactory for each of the purposes they are meant to serve.

I remember when the army decided to save on shelter-tent poles by issuing pup tents that were high at the shoulders and low at the rump, like a buffalo; a rifle was used for the front pole and a scabbarded bayonet for the rear pole. So what happened when both men in a tent had to go on guard? They took their rifles and bayonets with them, leaving their tent flat in the mud and rain.

Right now I'm trying to keep from inventing a hollow bamboo combination wading staff, rod case, and center pole for a pyramid tent. I'm also fighting the urge to invent a combination Dutch oven and pressure cooker, the two halves of which can also serve as a saucepan and a dishpan, respectively.

I am resisting these temptations by remembering not Sir Isaac Newton but old Nessmuk, who spent a lifetime camping. He was the high priest of the "go light" camping craze and was hipped on saving weight. But it's worth noting that he never used a single combination item in his home-designed and homemade equipment. If he needed a piece of equipment, he made it as light as possible. If he didn't need it—and mostly he didn't—he left it at home.

If you stick to that, you'll be able to pack a tent that's a real tent, a bed that's a real bed, an ax that's ax enough to do your work, and cooking utensils fit to prepare a bellyful of plain, nourishing grub. Carry the rest in your skull. Skill and knowledge weigh nothing, says Sir Isaac Newton.

CERTAIN BOYS

MOST NEW YORK ANGLERS KNOW THAT THE BRANCHES OF THE Croton River in Westchester and Putnam counties afford, in their short remaining links between a series of water-supply reservoirs, trout fishing of a sort (and sometimes a surprisingly good sort, too) for a horde of earnest anglers. During the first few weeks of the season one is sure of more company than he would like, but even in the late season one can be sure of finding someone to entertain and amuse him. So it is not surprising that my strongest recollections of the Croton are of neither water nor fish but of the people with whom I have fished or chatted. And of these the best were boys.

The first of these was Stevie, the son of an able angler, outstanding conservationist and all-round good fellow named Herman, whom we call the Judge. Stevie was quite a boy; for one thing, I thought on first meeting him that he was the only ten-year-old I had ever seen wearing a beard and moustache. Closer inspection revealed, however, that it was just the result of his steady feeding. He rose all day to cake, sand-wiches, fruit, hard-boiled eggs, pickles, and candy like a trout to a mayfly hatch; and, after all, a workman cannot do a job without cluttering up the workbench. Even though the Judge was of ample girth and capacity, I had thought three bushels of lunch would be too much for the three of us who had gone this day at the opening of the trout season to fish in Hemlock Reservoir. But I soon found I had to combine force with guile to get as much as a sandwich and an olive.

In those days a few smelt ran up into the West Branch of the Croton from Hemlock very early in the season, and the Judge and I had "dipped" a few by flashlight, the night before, for bait. They were enormous smelt, eight inches or more, and filled with vim and vigor. Always a sure-thing player, I had suggested that we take them home and eat them ourselves, but the Judge assured me our investment would produce large dividends if used as bait.

No friend of violent exercise, the Judge inclined to the method of fishing made famous by Rip Van Winkle. He sim-ply impaled a big hearty smelt on a bare hook and threw it off the bridge at the head of Hemlock to swim around and drum up business. He offered me one too, but I had the delusion that I could do better fishing with a bucktail up the inlet so as to meet the big fish returning to the reservoir after a night upstream with the smelt.

Stevie, surprisingly enough, had stopped feeding long enough to rig up a short steel rod with a sand-filled reel and a thick cotton line, and now he demanded a smelt. Loath to invest any of his precious racehorses in such an unlikely ven-ture, the Judge handed out a fish that was so nearly dead it was floating upside down in the pail; and although Stevie protested violently, that was what he had to take. So finally he hooked it on, chucked it in, and leaned his rod against the stone parapet of the bridge while he executed a flanking movement on two pounds of fudge.

Of course he had the right idea. His smelt wiggled feebly, and hence seductively, at long intervals instead of charging about and scaring away the trout, and he did not hold the rod. It is very important in still-fishing not to hold the rod, first because if you do, you send psychic waves down the line to warn the fish away, but more importantly, because if the angler is holding the rod he will inevitably strike too soon. The right time to strike in still-fishing is when the rod starts to go overboard.

Herman caught nothing and I caught nothing, but in about an hour Stevie's rod began to slide along the parapet and his reel to emit sounds suggestive of winding a dollar watch or mooring a ferryboat in its slip. Stevie rammed a banana into his mouth and grabbed the rod, and what followed was worth admission and amusement tax to witness. It was a triumph of deep hooking and good strong tackle over human nature, and a triumph of human nature over ethical concepts.

The Judge cast his rod aside and bounded in the air when he saw the bend Stevie was able to put in that steel rod without bringing the fish to the surface. And once in the air, he exploded in an impressive shower of vocabulary. Of course he was trying to help his son by giving him wise and useful directions, and probably any of his directions would have fallen in that category, but not all of them at once for they were mutually contradictory. If Stevie had tried to obey them, he would have lost his fish, and if he had allowed them to rattle him, he would have done the same. But this was a boy who knew the Judge, so he just ignored him and held on with might and main until his fish came splashing to the surface in all its awesome length and fury.

The actual sight of the fish destroyed whatever vestiges of self-control remained with the Judge. He unlimbered one of those snowshoe landing nets and clambered down the stone-work of the bridge, shouting to Stevie to lead the fish over so he could land it. Really, I thought the Judge was going to take a header into the icy water—he wasn't used to that sort of thing. But he made it. Then he went to work at netting the fish. Now I do not wish to traduce the Judge. I was a little distance off and maybe my eyes deceived me. But from where I stood he looked mightily like a man chopping down a tree. That must have been an awfully strong line.

But the fish's number was up, and the Judge finally netted it and lugged it up on the bridge. It was a most impressive brute; it weighed four pounds on the Judge's pocket scales, and three weeks later would have weighed six, for it was in thin, poor condition after its winter fasting. The Judge thrilled with paternal delight, his ethical concepts shone bright and clear, and his better nature was in the ascendant. He held the fish aloft and hailed me from the bridge:

"Hey! Look what Stevie caught!"

Alas for his better nature. This was a busy bridge on Opening Day and everyone knows the Judge. In a few minutes along came a car with rods sticking out of every window. The fishermen stopped to ask the Judge what luck.

"*We*," said the Judge, emphasizing the pronoun, "got a four-pounder," and he unveiled the fish dramatically. His better nature sagged at the knees at this sneak punch, but worse was to come. He had scarcely stowed the big fish back in his creel when another pole-sprouting car rattled across the bridge.

"Hey, Hoiman," bawled the driver in the accents of Brooklyn, "didja get sump'n'? I gotta four-pounder!"

The Judge peered into the proffered creel and his better nature went down for the count. Shoving Stevie into the bushes with one hand and drawing Stevie's trout like a saber with the other, he struck a heroic pose.

"*I* gotta *five*-pounder," he announced firmly, inelegantly, and untruthfully. So the Judge got the glory and all Stevie got was a bellyache.

The other boy who is connected with the Croton in my memory was a lad I met on the concrete embankment of the big pool below the railroad bridge in Croton Falls, as good a spot as the Café de la Paix for meeting anyone in the world. This was a little boy about eight years old who was wearing his father's rubber boots, with his shoes on inside them to make them fit. His legs were soaked because the boots leaked, and he was not fishing because he had lost his last hook in a huge trout that had cleaned him off.

"Does it make you feel bad to see all the others catching fish while you can't?" I asked, just to see what he would say. The answer was clear-strain and sporting, a little boy's unconscious rebuke.

"Oh, no," he said serenely. "Next to catching them myself I like to see other people catch them."

I wangled a bait hook for him and in return he gave me a little fly-rod lure that he had found stuck in the root on which his big fish cleaned him off. It was a humpbacked silver minnow half an inch long, the once-popular "Kensico Saw-belly," and I wore it in the band of my fishing hat for twenty years, until the hook rusted off and I lost it.

I had occasion to write to this boy subsequently—his name was Chuck Doyle—and got an acknowledgment from his mother. Ten years passed. And then, sometime around 1944, I got a letter from her saying she had found my name among some of Chuck's stuff and thought I might like to know where he was. He was a Marine, serving in an antiaircraft battery on Tinian Island. His older brother Phil was also a Marine, she told me; in fact, he had been one of that fabulous group, Edson's Raiders, throughout the terrible fighting on Guadalcanal.

One day the father of these two boys, with whom I had become acquainted, met me for lunch, and I learned that the older boy, Phil, had been wounded in the landing on Guam. He had written home from a convalescent center asking for a basketball, for they had worn out the only one they had—a sore deprivation for a boy who had played on all his high school teams and was particularly crazy about basketball. But it was wartime and, said his father sadly, there didn't seem to be a basketball left anywhere.

Naturally, I started hunting and by a lucky chance at last found a beauty, the Big League model. But the price was eighteen dollars, a lot of money in those days; Christmas was coming, and I was nearly broke as usual. So I told the clerk, "No, thank you," and then I remembered something.

Back a long time ago I paid a bellboy in Kansas City just eighteen dollars for a bottle of whisky so vile that after one drink I poured it down the sink. It had always weighed on my conscience, for in those days a whole family could have lived for a week on that sum, and there were plenty of families who could have used it. So I bought the basketball and shipped it to Phil, but I never heard from him.

Phil's outfit went to Okinawa. There his platoon became pinned down by heavy fire and reduced by many casualties. Phil, as platoon guide, unhesitatingly rushed across open terrain under intense small-arms fire and swam a deep irrigation ditch in order to inform his company commander of the desperate plight of his men. Then, leading a relief unit in a successful flanking movement, he rejoined his platoon and directed the evacuation of the many wounded. By his utter disregard for personal safety, his cool courage, and initiative, he was responsible for saving the lives of several of his comrades.

Not his own, though. Those aren't my words describing his exploit on Okinawa. They are from the citation that awarded the Silver Star posthumously to Sergeant Philip D. Doyle, L Company, Fourth Marines—young Phil Doyle of Croton Falls, New York.

It was years after the war before Mr. Doyle and I had one of our infrequent lunches together again. We talked of Phil and the boys, and the war, and I bragged of my skill in so carefully preparing and sending packages to servicemen that I had never lost a package in the mails. Then I remembered and said that there was one, for apparently Phil never had received the basketball I sent him. Mr. Doyle stared at me in astonishment.

"Didn't anyone ever tell you?" he demanded. "Phil wrote to us that he had received a splendid basketball from a man he didn't know, and they were having fun with it all day long. 'It never stops bouncing from morning to night,' he wrote."

I hardly ever think of that incident now except once in a while at night when I can't sleep and my sins of omission and commission crowd in on me. Then I put myself to sleep by thinking of that ball bouncing, bouncing . . . trying to calculate how many bounces per game, how many games per day, how many fine, brave young fellows had how much fun with that ball before they wore it out.

I might add that even at present prices there are a lot of bounces in a basketball and casts in a fishing rod per penny of cost, so if anyone wants to reduce his debit balance on the celestial books . . . See what I mean?

DOWN THE GREAT RIVER

DAWN WAS BREAKING ON THE GREAT RIVER. OUR CRAFT FLOATED far out on the vast expanse of hurrying waters, gliding past wooded bluffs and tangled, swampy shores. A mist overhung the river; only the lapping of the wavelets against our boat relieved the silence.

It was especially designed for the Great River, our boat; seven feet long and five wide, square-ended, it had a freeboard of two feet. It had a low bow and a high stern, over which was now draped a fabric that served us as a sail by day and a tent at night. Under it my partner Bill sprawled in sleep.

In the sweet coolness of early morning I jointed up a rod and cast out. A two-pound rainbow smashed at the fly.

"Fish for breakfast, Bill," I called gaily as the rod arched, and Bill emerged sleepily to seize the net and boat the fish. Together we laved faces and hands in the Great River.

But it was not to be fish that morning. Over the waters came a light craft propelled by a native woman who evidently wanted to barter with us. The natives of this section are still very friendly to explorers, so we beckoned her nearer and soon had acquired a variety of native foods which she bore— tropical fruits, "siryal," and the eggs of birds.

Breakfast over, I plunged in for a swim, forgetting the perils of the Great River; and so I experienced an adventure which might well have ended fatally. I was stroking along when a giant alligator broke water and made a dash for me. I struck out frantically for the boat, calling to Bill for aid, and to his quick response I owe my life. Snatching up a rifle, he sped a bullet into the saurian's brain, and we looped a rope over its jaws as it threshed in the water. It measured over twenty feet, a real man-eater.

Then the fishing began. The variety and size of our catch was almost unbelievable, for few flies have ever been cast in this stream. We took salmon, trout, and bass in profusion, fish to make an angler ecstatic. Occasionally we were surprised to land saltwater fish, sharks and tarpon and tuna, which apparently endure the river waters without discomfort. I doubt if anywhere in the world is there to be found such fishing as the Great River afforded us.

At intervals flights of ducks and geese appeared. Then we would muffle ourselves in our tent until their calls sounded overhead. "NOW!" I would cry and we would fling off the tent and fire into the massed birds with such deadly effect that they rained into the river around us.

We were hailing the shore to discover a native with whom we might trade for the noon meal when a tiger appeared on the bank. Usually these beasts slip quietly away, but this one swam out and attempted to board us. Again Bill saved the day, hitting it between the eyes with two slugs from a double-barreled shotgun, a deadly weapon at short ranges. As the beast slipped from the gunwale over which it had hooked its paws, I seized it, and together we got it aboard and whipped off the pelt. It was an enormous old male with worn and broken teeth, obviously a man-eater.

A lion which appeared immediately afterward met a better fate, for when he approached the boat we threw the tent over him, effectually muffling his teeth and claws, and hauled him aboard. Bill put a strap around his neck and soon tamed him so that he became our companion, sharing our rations, and spending most of his time in the boat.

Thus the day wore on, with a magnificent wild panorama of wooded banks continually unfolding. Rod and gun at hand, we reclined at ease while munching native "kukis" and "arnjes." When a breeze came up we rigged the tent as a sail and crested the waves at speed, Bill steering with a paddle. Rapid after rapid we shot without mishap, and once we even went over a falls, fortunately without shipping water.

As the sun declined, we ate a hot meal brought from a native village nearby, smoked our pipes, and prepared our staunch craft for the night. Dusk veiled the sky, and our sail came down to become a tent again. Side by side my partner and I sat by our little fire and discussed hunting, fishing, and other topics appropriate for explorers.

It had been a hard day. Exhausted by the ardors of combat and the chase, replete with nourishing fare, and lulled by the easy motion of the boat, my partner Bill slipped away from me into slumber.

Safe in his tent, a convalescent little boy with gold in his hair and cookie on his face smiled in his sleep as the shadowed banks of the Great River of Life swept unheeded past his bed, and a stout man with sparse grey hackles crept sheepishly down the stairs.

TAILPIECE TO A
FISHING TRIP

UNTIL AT LEAST AS RECENTLY AS 1930, THE OLD LUMBERING town of Chicoutimi, on the Saguenay River in Quebec, was isolated by land and had only the daily boat to Quebec for means of departure. So when the inhabitants married, the wedding trip necessarily began with an all-day boat ride to Quebec. And as the boat sailed at 7:00 A.M., the participants in a wedding had to arise at an unearthly hour, attend five o'clock Mass, hold the nuptial ceremony, and hurry through a real wedding breakfast before sailing time.

My wife and I and our old friend John Chabot were returning from a fishing trip. Our car was aboard the steamer and we were at the rail. We wondered at the size and animation of the crowd on the pier but not for long; whoops, shouts, and the sound of music announced the approach of a wedding party. In the core of it were the bride and groom battling their way through a dense mass of tearful, jovial, perspiring, wine-flushed, and excited relatives and friends, all bent on saying farewell.

The couple made the gangplank with something like a buck through tackle, went to their stateroom—one of a row all along both sides of the top deck, each with a window and door opening onto the deck and within, two bunks, and a washbasin in the corner—and emerged to take their places at the rail.

Now the witticisms came fast and furious, and John's translations were necessarily masterpieces of tact rather than accuracy, for the French are an uninhibited people and this was a situation made for their talents.

The departure whistle, however, soon cut short the witticisms and the efforts of an impromptu double quartet of the groom's pals. Silence fell as the lines were cast off, and the hidden ache of parting became plain to feel. A woman sobbed.

During all this time there was one who had stood silently apart. She was the bride's older sister, married and of course the mother of numerous children. Cowlike in figure and face, impassive and unmoving except for the mastication of a wad of gum, she had watched her sister unwinkingly ever since her first arrival at the rail. She had but one contribution to make, one gift to offer the bride, and not until the vessel stirred from the dock did she offer it.

Then, walking to the stringpiece, she spoke in a firm, carrying voice; earnestly serious, it was the veritable Voice of Experience.

"Rosie!"

"What?"

"Don't forget to pull down the shade!"

Then the boat sailed off into the sunrise amid a thundering, roaring salute of French-Canadian belly laughs.

Lady Beaverkill
Louise Brewster Miller

Herman Christian, with the rod Gordon gave him (now in the collection of The Anglers' Club of New York). In the several years during which Gordon boarded with Anson Knight, Christian was his nearest neighbor and most frequent fishing companion. Christian, Roy Steenrod, and the late Bruce Leroy were Gordon's three angling familiars in the Catskills.

◀

Theodore Gordon on the Neversink, probably ca. 1912.

Two great American angling pioneers: George Michel
Lucien LaBranche (left), *The Dry Fly and Fast Water* and
The Salmon and the Dry Fly; and Edward Ringwood
Hewitt (right), *Telling on the Trout, Secrets of the
Salmon, Handbook of Stream Improvement, Handbook of
Fly Fishing,* and other books. From the etchings by Gordon
Stevenson.

Herman Christian's development of Gordon's Bumblepuppy. Shown here in its exact size, it is considered unsurpassed as a night fly for the biggest brown trout; with it Waldemar Kesk once won the *Field & Stream* national contest for biggest brown trout, thirteen pounds. Despite its size (1/0 Model Perfect), it has the trim, clean, spare appearance typical of the Catskill tie.

◀

The Hendrickson, created by Roy Steenrod to imitate the female of *Ephemerella subvaria*. Its tremendous success and popularity on most American brown trout waters currently rank it above the Quill Gordon. The fly is shown here in Theodore Gordon's vise, which Steenrod still uses. **Actual size is No. 12.**

The narrow exit of the Big Bend Pool on the Neversink in summer low water. A short cast to the left of this angler, there is eight to ten feet depth of water along the rocky bank. This magnificent pool still exists unchanged on that part of the old Hewitt water above the City's "take line" for LaGuardia (now Neversink) Reservoir, which is leased by The Big Bend Club.

▶

Right up to the time the bulldozers came in to build the reservoir, this was a familiar sight on the Hewitt water four or five times every day of the season—Ed assuaging his passion for angling. This typical Neversink pool now sleeps under sixty feet of water.

The Theodore Gordon Society and some distinguished friends: (*left to right*) Sparse Grey Hackle (The Reporter); Guy Jenkins (The Underwriter); John McDonald, whose book *The Complete Fly Fisherman: The Notes and Letters of Theodore Gordon* rescued Gordon from oblivion; Roy Steenrod, Gordon's closest friend; Virginia Kraft, a peerless researcher; the late Edgar G. Wandless (The Attorney); and Lewis M. Hull (The Physicist).

Gateway to a half-acre of seemly peace and simple dignity still remote from the ugliness, grime, sordid poverty, and squalor that surround it.

The laurel was for Fanny, too.

The DeBruce Fly-Fishing Clubhouse; its water includes the famous Ward stretch of the Willowemoc at DeBruce, New York. The pond takes water from the Willowemoc above the club dam, returns it below. Generations of frustrated beaver, vainly trying to raise the pond level by damming its outlet, keep the club fireplace supplied.

▶

Spring high water; the foam marks the entry of the Little Mongaup into the Junction Pool of the Willowemoc on the old Ward water. Here George LaBranche cast his first "dry fly" as related in *The Dry Fly and Fast Water,* his classic work which in 1915 launched the dry fly in America and remains a foundation stone of angling literature.

Chester Cairns took his machinery across the Beaverkill on this long diagonal ford at the foot of Cairns' Pool to mow his fields on the opposite bank, leaving white wheel marks on the algae-covered brown stones. The present writer therefore christened the hitherto anonymous pool below the ford "The Wagon Tracks." The exposed bottom in the middle of the ford was under two feet of water in midsummer, before the road builders came.

The Lamp, the true symbol of the lotus eaters of the Brooklyn
Fly Fishers.

Harry Darbee on the Margaree.

A DRINK OF WATER

NO ONE RAISED AS I WAS IN GREATER NEW YORK HAS ANY REAL awareness of drinking water until he gets beyond access to the pure, bountiful, never-failing supply which blesses that city. So when the New York militia division went to Texas on the Mexican Border Patrol, we were shocked and dismayed to find that not only was the water saturated with earth chemicals—Epsom salts, as a matter of fact—so that it was well-nigh undrinkable, but so scarce that on occasion it was an article of purchase and sale.

Small wonder that when the Sixty-ninth Infantry, the Fighting Irish, marched to Laguna Seca and found a native Texan waiting there to sell them water at ten cents a canteenful because the windmill well-pump was "broken," they chased him into the brush with fixed bayonets, cut out of harness and drove away his mules, confiscated his water, smashed the barrels, and burned the wagon. To men who as boys had followed the universal New York custom of ringing the nearest doorbell and asking for a drink of water when they were thirsty, it was revolting that there should be a price on water.

We learned about water, down there. We learned after a mass epidemic of bellyaches not to ice it. We learned that water from a mile of piping laid aboveground, exposed to a 130-degree sun temperature, would quench thirst better than if it were cold. We learned to drink soldierly from a canteen by admitting air from the side of the mouth, and to drink at the trot without knocking out our front teeth, by propping the thumb firmly against the chin for a steady-rest. We even enjoyed learning those things because we were very young.

Some of us learned to husband our water by drinking sparingly on the march, but the rookies didn't, so Davy Baldwin and I, caisson corporals of the fifth and sixth sections, were worried for our men when orders came for a thirty-mile march to the artillery target range at Monte Cristo Ranch, for we knew it would be a dry march. We agreed to carry two extra canteens apiece for our men but to drink none ourselves, to set a good example. Instead, we would chew tobacco. We had learned that deplorable habit from being around horses, for smoking is properly a deadly sin anywhere around a stable or even an outdoors picket line.

We made the march, as I recall, in some twelve hours, every step of the way at a walk through rolling clouds of alkali dust so dense one could not see the gun carriage ahead. Each man had his quart canteen and there was half a cup of cold coffee at the noon halt. But that afternoon our drivers were in distress, and it was well that we had an extra pint of water per man to dole out to them. Davy and I chewed stoically; and when camp was made we each rode four horses bareback into the hurly-burly around the watering tank just to show how tough we were. As I said, we were young. Then we came to the best drink I ever had.

You can grow anything in that country if you have water, and Sterling's Ranch had some seven-hundred-foot wells. Sterling raised citrus fruit in a small way, and that afternoon he had a whole barrel of fresh-fruit limeade in a shady spot, selling it for a nickel a pint canteen cupful. Still sitting our water-bloated and weary horses, Davy and I blew the dust off our lips, licked away the mud, raised our cups to each other, and then dumped them down our throats with a single motion. It merely tasted cool. The second cup went down right after it, again with a single lift. It tasted cool and wet. We grinned at each other across the third cup and poured it down the hatch to join the others, and for the first time we tasted the flavor of limes. Then with our fourth cup in hand we booted our weary horses out of the way and sipped the delightful draft—four gulps instead of one. It is inconceivable to me now that a skinny young man of 147 pounds could drink two measured quarts of liquid in five minutes, but I did and no bellyache either. Must have been the tobacco that saved me. Or maybe I was just young.

Because of what the army taught me, I am no friend of surface water; I won't drink from any stream that has any human habitation on its watershed. And I'm suspicious of rural wells. A farm well is usually at the lowest point in the landscape but surprisingly often the privy is on the highest, and sometimes so is the barnyard manure pile. Just the smell of some of those old wells is enough to convince you that there is something in them besides water. If I have to use such water, I boil or chlorinate it first. Even the sparkling spring deserves to have its antecedents considered. One of my friends got typhoid from a lovely sparkling spring which, tests with soluble dyes later proved, flowed right through the mountain from a polluted area in the next valley. If all this sounds old-maidish and timid, I will remind you that I have not yet had typhoid.

But when you go into the deep woods, you come to the very best kind of drinking that there is. And you enjoy it all the more because nothing builds up a deep, insistent thirst like carrying a heavy pack through close, unstirring second growth on a broiling, humid August day. Your clothes become cemented to you, the packstraps emboss your tender skin, the hot touch of the pack itself raises prickly heat on your back, and your glasses slide around on your streaming face.

Then, just as your knees start trembling and you begin to see little black spirals before your eyes, you come to an icy trickle, bubbling and murmuring over bright pebbles. You discard your reeking hat and foggy glasses, drop to your knees and then to all fours, and then you lower yourself, pack and all, onto your belly and drink like a horse.

I use that simile because a horse really enjoys his water. He can be dainty enough when he is not very thirsty, shoving floating dust aside with his muzzle and playing with the water. But a horse that has walked thirty miles under a blazing Texas sun shoves his long face in right up to the eyes, and you can see gulps of water as big as oranges chasing each other down his throat. When he has to come up for air he snorts and shakes his head and throws water all around, then resumes drinking until he sloshes and gurgles internally. Then he turns away, luxuriously chewing his last mouthful of water and letting it run out of his mouth and down his chin.

So you drink like a horse, cooling your face in the water, until you come up gasping and snorting. As you lie there flat on your belly you put your hands and wrists into the icy flow and not until they begin aching do you climb to your feet, a new man.

The prettiest drinking place that I remember was on Finch & Pruyn's timber reserves in the Adirondacks on which we were trespassing to fish the Rock River, long ago. This was the deep cathedral woods. Right beside our camp was a tiny spring. Water seeped from under the dead leaves, trickled over a mossy stone and fell from the emerald fringe, a drop at a time, into a pebbly basin that held just enough to fill a coffeepot or a very thirsty fisherman. As it fell, each drop sounded a different note, so that the spring continually played a chime of little silver bells. One scarcely noticed it by day, but in the stillness of the night the wood sprites played faint elfin tunes on it, ineffably sweet and clear. No wonder the bucks came down in the moonlight to cut up their stamping ground with their hoofs, and the beavers worked on their dam so close we could hear the falling of trees and the slapping of broad tails. It was an enchanted place.

But the saddest drinking place I remember was on Ed Hewitt's Neversink. He had five princely miles of that river, the most wildly beautiful stream I ever saw. It was brilliantly clear. ("The water is lucent as air," Theodore Gordon wrote.) It ran over white sand and granite stones through a narrow forested valley, a place of rugged bristling steeps, moss-hung rock faces, brawling rapids, and deep blue pools. So wild it seemed that one expected any moment to see the painted, feathered head of a Mohawk rise stealthily among the alders. On a bench extending into the largest of the valley meadows stood an old farmhouse, which Ed called The Camp, and here his "rods," who rented annual fishing privileges, used to gather after the day's fishing was over for unforgettable nights of fun and companionship. It was the last of the Golden Age.

Then New York City took most of Hewitt's stream for a reservoir and came in with bulldozers to remove every tree and bush and blade of grass right up to the projected waterline of the reservoir, and even to alter the contours of the valley, leaving a wasteland of desecrated, barren ground.

It was 110 degrees by the thermometer on Ed Hewitt's mountain-top porch that August afternoon when I walked down the breakneck trail into the valley to see what the bulldozers had done. In the Biblical phrase, it was the abomination of desolation. The river was shrunken, the pools bulldozed into narrow channels among bare, rough stones and sterile dirt that held the heat like the lining of a blast furnace. As I climbed up onto what was left of the elevated spur of land, I couldn't even be sure just where the Camp had been.

Then I heard running water. The bulldozers had leveled the Camp and filled in the foundation, all but one corner, and in that was the spring which the original builder had taken pains to include in his cellar. I climbed down into the crevice and found protruding from the foundation wall a pipe from which poured a strong, lively stream, clear as air and cold as ice, the only living thing in that valley of silent ruin. Beside it was a champagne bottle—what other fishing camp boasted champagne?—and I chilled the thick green glass before I filled it.

Then I had a drink better than any champagne, a drink

from the old Camp spring—a drink all alone save for the friendly and approving spirits of as fair a company of good angling companions as ever existed. I raised the bottle high and toasted the good old days in their behalf.

Then I climbed out and went up the river, past the Camp Pool and Molly's Pool and the Shop Pool; the Flat Pool, the Long Pool, York's Ford, the Island Pool—or rather, the places where they had been—and up to the Little Bend and the Big Bend. As I walked, salty drops ran down my face; but they were just perspiration. Just perspiration.

CHANCE MEETINGS

DURING NEARLY HALF A CENTURY OF FLY FISHING I HAVE OF course encountered a veritable host of fishermen. Some were great figures of angling, some were as able with pen as with rod, most were anonymous, conventional types—good-hearted, friendly, helpful, kindly "regular fellows." But a few had something unique or at least unusual about them that has made them linger in my memory. Most were encountered by chance and my contact with them was fleeting or no more than brief. Others became warm acquaintances; a few, friends.

They were a diverse lot; if they had anything approaching a common characteristic, it was the way they had come into fishing. The most unlikely types, city born and city bred without even the remotest previous contact with fishing, suddenly conceived a passion to go fishing, assembled equipment, and forthwith went, all without seeking counsel or even taking a preliminary dip into the literature of the sport. Their utter inability to explain how they got interested in fishing and their great valor of ignorance are the only things they had in common. Let us look at a few of them.

The Fuller Brush Man. One of the most unusual fishermen in my experience I met on the Big Beaverkill on a hot, fishless Fourth of July weekend. There was a man in the head of this long pool, so I went down to the tail to fish wet through the rift. Presently he walked down and spoke pleasantly and courteously.

"This is supposed to be a good rod, but it won't cast," he said. "Would you tell me what is the matter with it?"

Part of the matter was that he couldn't cast and part was a line one size too light, but the main thing was that the line had perished and gone sticky. I greased it and rubbed it down, but it was gone.

"I'm up for three days; can I get another line around here?" he asked. In those days every store on Main Street, Roscoe, except the undertaker's, sold tackle, so the answer was yes.

"Then will you have breakfast with me tomorrow and help me pick a new line?" he invited. And I did.

This man—his name escapes me now—had an unusual history. He had been an infantry top sergeant in the First World War and had learned automobile service work in an Army of Occupation school. He became service manager of the Packard Agency in Englewood, New Jersey, an excellent position and with employers of whom he spoke in the highest terms.

Nevertheless, he was unhappy, restless, became unable to sleep well, could not eat regularly, lost weight, and suffered from nervousness. One morning, on a sudden impulse, he resigned his job. He was an excellent man and his employers did not want to lose him, so they offered him a large rise in pay, a vacation to rest up in, or whatever he wanted to make him happy, but he refused.

He went back to his rooming house, decided he ought to look for another job, and found a classified advertisement through which he became that familiar figure, the Fuller Brush Man. For ninety-nine men out of a hundred, door-to-door canvassing is a soul-corroding experience, but he was the hundredth man. Immediately he began ringing doorbells his appetite returned, he was able to sleep soundly, and he began to put on weight. And he was successful from his first day. When I met him he had been doing this work for two years, had been advanced to the position of supervisor, and was the most completely happy man in his work that I have ever seen.

In some manner that he was entirely at a loss to explain, he had developed an interest in fishing, and yet this was the first time he had actually gone fishing—probably because it was his first vacation in two years.

"Would you like to see my tackle?" he asked. Now this was no shrinking violet but a real man, an infantry topkick with combat experience, a boss who could control rough mechanics, and a man with the courage and fiber not only to withstand but actually to gain stimulation from the succession of rebuffs that assail a canvasser all day long. Yet the way in which he issued this invitation had something so boyish and confiding in it that I felt as if he had exposed a defenseless side of himself to me, knowing that I would not hurt him.

He was staying in a little wooden shack behind Tillie Schmidt's boardinghouse beside the Summer House Pool, and

I tell you that except for a cot and a washstand the place looked like a tackle shop. He had three army footlockers crammed to the top, and any number of tin tackle boxes and shoulder bags hung or stacked all over the place.

You never saw such a collection in your life, and when I read years later, in the Theodore Gordon letters, of Gordon's ambition to collect one of every item of tackle offered for sale in the American market, I thought at once of my Fuller Brush Man. He had done it.

About 90 percent of it was freshwater tackle, but beyond that there was no discrimination. He had, I am sure, one of every kind of plug and lure ever offered to anglers, any number of reels both fly and bait, a few rods, and just one fly line; and he had heaps and piles and masses of the incidentals that fishermen use: flies, leaders, clippers, disgorgers, boxes, sandals, nets, minnow pails—everything but books.

The explanation was simple but astonishing. He assured me that in two years of being on the streets all day every day, he had never—*never*—passed a tackle store without going in and buying something. And yet, as I said, this was his first fishing trip. He couldn't spare the time, he confided; when he was not supervising his crew he was out selling, himself, to keep his hand in.

He was an awfully nice fellow, and we had fun together for a couple of days even though we didn't catch a thing. We talked a lot about the army and, particularly, about his work. We even became so friendly that he was moved to confess to me how he once had almost committed a sin. He had been tempted to walk past a house without knocking (it had no bell) because it was so mean and squalid and in such a poor neighborhood. In fact, he *had* walked past it. But then his conscience assailed him and he turned back and knocked. And sold fifty dollars' worth of brushes to an aged Italian woman who couldn't speak English, he assured me with the air of a man who had attained salvation through repentance and good works.

I suggested that we keep in touch, but he didn't know when he would be able to go fishing again, he worked evenings ("You make some of your best sales then"), and he never came to New York. I'd still like to see him again.

The Scrapper. Another man who became a fisherman in this mysterious way is Eli, a financial newspaperman I used to see in the course of my work. One evening I went into the old United Press newsroom. One of the fellows was up on a chair wielding a long window pole, and when he saw me he yelled, "Hey, Deac!" and began making casting motions with it. It drew a general laugh—my interest in fishing is pretty well known in the fraternity—and then one of the deskmen looked up and said, "Hey, Deac! I want to ask you something." He walked out into the hall with me and continued, "I've taken up fishing lately. I can cast plugs a little, but I can't make the fly rod work. Can you help me?" So I made a date forthwith to take him up on Boyd's Corners Reservoir for instruction.

Eli's story was unusual and interesting. His father was a rabbi. As a schoolboy the necessity of preserving his existence in the jungles of The Bronx made him learn to defend himself, and he became extremely handy with his dukes; in fact, sparring was a hobby with him. He played high-school football and was very good at it.

When he went to work he tried "club" (semipro) football on weekends as a source of exercise and an outlet for his energies, but he found it was impossible to keep in good enough condition to diminish the risk of injury. So for several years he found diversion in going around from one neighborhood saloon to another, looking for "friendly fights" with anyone who fancied himself and felt like a good-natured go with the maulies.

I must emphasize that Eli was as far as possible from being a bully and was not truculent or overbearing; he simply looked for, and found, kindred spirits who could enjoy giving and taking a few good ones in the spirit of fun and frolic which characterizes the Manly Art of Self-Defense at its best. Not that Eli couldn't fight when he had to. There probably still are a few chaps in the UPI (as it is now) who remember the time Eli wrecked a desk, a typewriter, and an opponent with a single punch when one of his men resented a reprimand by taking a swing at him.

This is an accurate portrayal, and I cannot imagine a man less likely to be attracted to the gentle, solitary sport of angling. Yet he, like the Fuller Brush Man, became interested in it in some manner which he was totally unable to explain; he bought Sears-Roebuck fly- and bait-casting outfits complete and went on his vacation up on the Big Beaverkill —in August.

He learned to get out a plug fairly well, but, he confided, he could not cast a fly. So he tied a leader and a fly to a plug and cast the whole thing out, an ingenious solution which I am not sure yet may not have some merit. But he didn't catch any of the numerous trout he saw. "They didn't run away but they wouldn't bite," he told me. "They must have seen me." And I didn't have the heart to tell him about those huge Beaverkill suckers.

When it came to the casting lesson, I figured that as good an athlete as Eli would have conditioned reflexes and also the ability to analyze motions and isolate the fundamentals. So I told him the idea, demonstrated a few times, and handed him the rod. It was something to see. His second try was a cast, and before he had been at it a quarter of an hour he was laying down short but clean and straight casts, and his timing was better than mine. I took him fishing a time or two to give him perspective and some comprehension of the fundamentals, and after that his natural ability, self-confidence, and energy enabled him to take it from there. In no time at all he was a reasonably competent fisherman and was beginning to "discover" the less-popular fishing waters.

Eli left the wire service, and I see him now only very occasionally if I attend the Financial Writers annual show, but at our last encounter he was still an active, devoted, and successful fisherman who obviously had already passed most of the milestones along the upward path of the sportsman angler.

The Man Who Broke Seth Green. There is one man whom I certainly wouldn't remember if he had not been connected with a great figure in American fishing history, for it is forty-five years ago that I was reading a fishing-tackle catalog on a commuting train and a sour-faced elderly man beside me remarked on it.

"I knew Seth Green," he volunteered. "He was a miller up near Rochester, New York, and I was a boy on a farm nearby. That was almost at the end of the Civil War, and wheat and flour had soared to tremendous prices. Seth contracted with every farmer in the vicinity to buy wheat at those levels, and then the approaching end of the war knocked the bottom out of flour prices. I was only ten years old, but I was the man of the family while my father was in the army, and I was running the farm. I was hurrying to get my wheat in, fearing Green might run out of money, when I got a tip from town that he was in serious financial difficulties. I sent the women and children out into the fields to rush the last of the harvesting, loaded my wheat right away, and drove as fast as I could to Green's mill and demanded my contract price, which of course was by then far above the market. Green looked pretty sick and said I would have to wait a couple of hours while he got the money.

" 'Take this fishing rod and go down along the edge of the mill pond and do some trout fishing to amuse yourself while you wait,' he coaxed me. 'There are some real big ones in there; Seth Green's babies, I call 'em.'

"I went down along the pond," continued the elderly man, "and by the time Green came back with the money I had five beautiful three-pound brook trout. I went home with fifteen pounds of fish and over three hundred dollars. That was the last money he paid out.

"So," he concluded with a smirk of self-satisfaction, "I'm the man who busted Seth Green."

I was not very sorry to observe that he was so seedy looking as to give the impression that he had not prospered in the long run, and I have often reflected without enthusiasm on the character of a man who could "bust" his neighbor, hog his splendid trout, and boast of the whole performance.

The Paratrooper. My wife once belonged to a women's fishing club that leased a clubhouse and some water on a Catskill stream, and this time we were fishing there with our daughter Patty.

We were surprised to receive, on our first evening, a call from a most personable young man, a paratrooper just out of the service, who was our neighbor by virtue of living two miles up the road. He knew two other members of the club who were also staying at the house and his call was ostensibly on them.

But within five minutes he had executed a turning movement and realigned his advance with us as his objective. Then he put down the best directed and most skillfully laid barrage I ever saw, so well organized that we did not recognize it as a holding action. He was awaiting an anticipated tactical development, but when it did not materialize he finally had to make a frontal attack.

"Where is your daughter, Miss Pat?" he asked with a most charming smile. "I hear she is very pretty." He glowed like a neon sign.

"She's in bed," said Lady Beaverkill.

"In bed!" exclaimed Airborne in shocked surprise. "But it's only nine o'clock."

"Well, she's only nine years old," said my wife mildly.

He never dimmed his smile or flicked an eyelid, but behind him the two ladies developed severe cases of internal mirth. I didn't learn until afterward that, chancing to meet Airborne that morning, they had told him we were coming up with our pretty daughter; but either by accident or, more likely, design they had omitted the very vital statistic.

Airborne had had it but, like all paratroopers, he was a master of minor tactics. In five minutes he had cleared his flanks, disengaged his forward elements, and was falling back under heavy covering fire to a previously prepared position. But the last volley to ring in his ears as he started his half-hour walk home in the darkness was the pealing laughter of his unsympathetic acquaintances.

The Novice. I was coming out of the tail of Cairns' Pool one time on my way to an early dinner when I spotted a fish rising close against the bank. It took the gray variant I offered and immediately proved itself to be a lowly eight-inch stocker, which was quickly netted and released.

"Congratulations! You played him very nicely," said a pleasant voice above and behind me, the voice of a young man who had been watching me from the edge of the road. Since neither the fish nor the handling had merited congratulations, I deduced that this was a novice but also a man of goodwill and sportsmanlike instincts.

He proved me right. It was his first day astream, with an outfit he had bought complete in a discount store, on impulse and without knowing why. Luck had been with him; he had had a wonderful day. His outfit had proved adequate if not fancy; he hadn't been able to cast with his new fly rod, of course, but he had let his big wet flies run down in the current; and wonder of wonders, he had caught three fish. And now he was on his way back to the hotel, at peace with the world, but had stopped to watch when he saw me hang my little fish.

"Would you like to see my trout?" he asked, hauling a canvas creel from his car and drawing forth three small fish. Right then I faced a decision which I still wonder whether I made correctly. But as I still see it, I had either to well-nigh break his heart then or let someone else do it later; I could just imagine him displaying his catch to the fishermen in the Antrim Lodge bar.

"Look," I said gently. "There is one mark by which you can always identify a trout. Every trout has it and no other fishes have," and I explained about the adipose fin.

"What are these, then?" he asked.

"Chub," I told him, and explained about chub.

"Then I suppose I might as well throw these away," he said miserably, his happy day ruined. I did the best I could.

"Why did you come all the way up here just to go fishing?" I demanded. "It was to have fun, wasn't it?"

"Yes; of course."

"Well, didn't you have fun when you caught those fish?"

"I certainly did!" he said firmly and even smiled for an instant at the recollection.

"Then you got what you came for; you had fun. And you learned something very important. You learned that it's not fish that make the sport but just catching them—or even just trying to catch them."

He seemed to look a little less disconsolate as he drove away, but maybe that was just my wishful thinking. I still wonder whether I made the right decision.

The Compleat Sportsman. Les Shaw was a slight, quiet but colorful chap with whom I fished all through the Catskills one hilarious season in my two-cylinder Crosley. Rather than take a job in his father's woodworking plant ("too dangerous; I saw too many fingers cut off") he ran away from home. Then he and another sixteen-year-old somehow managed to buy a steam-powered racing automobile from the widow of the driver whom it had killed. With it they joined an itinerant group of auto racers which campaigned among the county fairs and dirt trotting tracks of the South. The boys' car was twice as fast as the others, but entirely uncontrollable on turns, which abound on small dirt tracks; but that, he assured me, was not dangerous.

"Our principal danger was starvation," he said. "We lived on Dr. Pepper soda pop and doughnuts; the rest of our occasional winnings went for new racing tires."

Thereafter he became, successively, a railroad locomotive fireman, a clerk in the Boston & Maine repair shops, an accountant, a financial reporter for *United States Investor* magazine, and the best railroad bond analyst I ever knew. He was a member of a United States Government commission that surveyed German railroad damage from Allied bombing in World War II, and he was expecting appointment to the Interstate Commerce Commission when he died untimely.

Mostly he fished with his wife, a lovely woman whom he called his Best Girl Friend, who was not an angler but a bird watcher. I have heard so often his story of a chance meeting that befell them at the old DeBruce Club Inn that I feel as if it were mine by inheritance.

As he told it, he was fishing this day above the old bridge at DeBruce when he noted that it was time to haul out for dinner, and beckoned to his wife, who was bird-watching on the bridge and talking to a chap who was fishing over the railing. When she joined Les, she said the chap claimed to be a deer hunter, and added, "I hope he knows more about deer than he does about birds; he called a flicker a brown woodpecker."

A moment later the deer hunter ran to his car, which was parked beside theirs, exclaiming, "There's a hatch of Royal Coachmen on; I saw a trout take one."

He pawed through his gear and came up with a huge No. 4 Coachman—wet, of course. Les offered him a choice of smaller sizes, but he elected to use his own. What he did want, though, was information about the water, so Les told him about the eddy under the tree roots and the hole in back of the abutment. As he expressed thanks and took off for the bridge again, Les expressed the hope that he knew more about deer than he did about stream insects.

Just as they were finishing dinner at the inn, the deer hunter came up to their table with beaming countenance.

"I got him!" he said. "Right in the hole where you told me. Biggest trout I ever caught. You folks are leaving, ain't you? I want you to take the trout home with you."

Les protested but the chap ended the argument with a bow to the Best Girl Friend and a firm pronouncement. "Please, I want her to have it. I put it on the seat of your car in a paper bag. Good-bye and good luck."

When they were ready to leave, Les looked into his car and there was the fish, all eleven inches of it. He thought of the warm friendliness and the generosity which had impelled this true sportsman to bestow the biggest trophy he had ever caught for so small a favor as a little information. He stowed it on the front seat between them, and his Best Girl Friend smiled approvingly.

"We'll drop it in the Neversink for my pet blue heron," she said. "He loves chub."

Flytiers in Left Field. Back in the days when Charlie Kerlee was one of the very best commercial photographers in New York, I stopped by to say hello to him. He had a girl on the model stand, and you will believe that she was a toothsome dish when I say that she was the highest-priced fashion model at that time and, I believe, the first to receive one hundred dollars an hour for her work. She was wearing a gorgeous fur coat, which was being brushed meticulously by the furrier who owned it so as to get the right play of light on it. (Of course, such "props" are borrowed; the owner takes the publicity for his pay.)

Then entered a mutual friend who was a dedicated amateur flytier. At the sight of this fur-clad lovely he stopped short and pointed like a bird dog, then bounded forward with a glad cry.

"Wow!" he exclaimed. "What a gorgeous body . . ." The model jerked her head around to slay another fresh guy with a dagger look, but the newcomer ignored her to fondle a corner of the coat while he finished his exclamation. "What a gorgeous body that would spin into!"

Just in case these lines are read by someone who is not familiar with the flytier's method of constructing an artificial fishing fly, I will explain that the tier sometimes "spins"—twists—clipped fur around a sticky silk thread and then winds the furry thread in close turns around the shank of a fishhook to make a body for his imitation of an insect.

"What is it?" continued the flytier as he gazed at the glorious, creamy, cinnamon-tinged fur.

"Fisher," said Charlie. "*Only* twelve thousand dollars."

"Yeah?" said the unimpressed flytier. "Gosh, I wish I could get just a little piece of it."

"I could give you a few trimmings," said the amused furrier.

"You can? Oh, boy! Thanks!" chortled the flytier, almost beside himself, and hastily hauled out his business card.

As we walked out together I remarked, "That girl is really a cupcake, isn't she?"

"What girl?" demanded the flytier vaguely. "Gee, I hope that guy remembers to send me those clippings. What a body!"

I have known, and known of, flytiers who were farther out in left field than that. For instance: For some years during and after World War II, a chap named Harlan Maynard, an accomplished amateur tier, worked as a volunteer to teach flytying to disabled veterans at Halloran General Hospital on Staten Island, New York. This hard-fisted, hard-faced, hard-talking, and soft-hearted Maine man had a magnetic personality, and his classes tied with a fanatical fervor that persisted after they had been discharged and sent home. He once showed me letters from two of his grateful graduates, the following extracts from which illustrate my point.

Wrote one: "I am back to tying. I want to get a dozen of each size of twenty patterns in time for the opening of the trout season. My wife gave birth to a boy yesterday, nine pounds. I have picked up a very promising pointer pup and am training him, but most of the time I tie flies. . . ."

Wrote the other: "I sure miss the class and wish I were back tying with you. I am getting tools and materials to start again. My wife went out for the evening three days ago and hasn't come back yet. Wait till she gets home. How are all the fellows in the class? I have found a place with some good blue necks and the price is right too. . . ."

But I think the most in flytiers was the chap who came into the smoking compartment of a Pullman sleeper one night when the late Walter Sill of The Anglers' Club of New York was using a portable flytying kit to tie salmon flies to while away the time.

"Thunder and Lightning!" said the young man, which was not an exclamation but the name of the fly Walter was tying. He sat down to talk, and in half an hour the porter came in.

"Your wife sent me to see where you were, suh," he said.

"Tell her I'll be right back," said the young man. Half an

hour later, while they were taking turns at the tying vise, the porter returned. He addressed the young man again.

"Your wife says to come back, suh," he said.

"Right away," said the young man, waxing another piece of thread and never looking up.

Half an hour and two salmon flies later the porter returned for the third time.

"Your wife says to come right away, suh," he said.

"I guess I'll have to leave you," the young man said with an apologetic smile, "or my wife will be sore at me. You see, we were married just this afternoon."

He was a *real* flytier.

The Singers. It was a time of gloom and sorrow, for the disaster at Pearl Harbor and the hopeless plight of our troops on Bataan cast down our spirits. The military had refused me firmly and there was little I could do to help, so I went fishing, as I could after I discovered that a 1940 Ford would run on unrationed kerosene

Thus it was that early one Saturday morning in August my wife and I, on our way to the Beaverkill, encountered on the forward deck of the Newburgh ferryboat a group of men enjoying the rising sun and cool breeze on their way to work in the war plants across the Hudson.

Clad in scrubbed, faded blue bib overalls and blue denim shirts, they were middle-aged men with gray hair and comfortable waistlines but with wide shoulders too and strong, calloused hands. One of them reminded me of my Uncle Frank, who had the front of a buffalo and a handlebar moustache all across his broad Saxon face; who could lift anything he could get a good hold of, and, besides, made the most marvelous wooden guns for my cousin and me to hunt deer and bears all along the fencerows of the old farm.

They did not mind being up early or going to work on a Saturday, those men, but joked and laughed together, and I think they must have been members of some sort of singing society or chorus, for several times during the long trip they broke into snatches of harmony of which they sang but a few bars each time before lapsing into mirth and banter.

The ferryboat came into the slip and made fast. The gates went up. The group started off the boat. Then suddenly one of them raised a strong baritone voice.

"Onward, Christian soldiers . . ." he sang, and the others came in with a heart-stopping crash:

"MARCHING AS TO WAR!"

On the instant they were all in step, pounding their heels on the planking and swinging their tin dinner pails in unison to the cadence of the greatest marching song ever written.

Through the cavernous, echoing ferry shed and out onto the cobbles of the old river town they went, still singing, in an irregular formation that somehow reminded me of skirmishers going forward under fire. As I eased the car past them, the one who looked like Uncle Frank stopped singing a moment and smiled as he saw the aluminum rod cases stacked in the back of the car.

"Good luck," he said, and I seemed to hear Uncle Frank add, "Olfurd," as he always used to pronounce my name in the old-fashioned country way.

My heart was uplifted, and suddenly all was made clear to me.

"They'll never beat us; *never!*" I exclaimed. "Men like that made America great; men like that will keep her great."

And so they did.

MINOR MYSTERIES

I SUPPOSE EVERY ANGLER HAS A SMALL ACCUMULATION, IN HIS fly box or merely in memory, of flies about which he is doomed to puzzle and speculate forevermore. They are the flies which were fantastically effective, once and once only. He was mystified by their success and he is enraged at their subsequent failure. I have four of them in mind.

One was a marabou streamer tied long and slim to imitate a minnow. Because the utterly limp marabou feather responds in slow water to the slightest rod-tip movement with a deadly, realistic wag of its tail, it has long been my favorite for casting to minnowing fish. I therefore resorted to the marabou one summer when I had a rod on water stocked with huge fish that turned to minnowing after the hatches were off. The fish, the close brush, and my own brand of casting soon combined to deprive me of all the white marabous I had. So I acquired the only marabou streamer in the village store, reluctantly since it was dyed an incredible shade of orange.

Notwithstanding my little faith in it, this gewgaw made me the master of the river; I commanded the fish like a god. In fact, it was so good that I decided to save it from the fate of its predecessors and preserve it for a pattern. Then a dealer to whom I gave it to match lost it—he said. And the store-keeper who had sold it to me couldn't remember where he had bought it.

For years, every conceivable shade (and many inconceivable ones) of marabou that I could purchase or dye, from palest lemon to darkest burnt orange, was painstakingly tested on that same water and those same fish—everyone caught and released them times without number. Not one of all those streamers was worth a damn, except to adorn a hatband and pleasure the ladies.

*   *   *

I make stonefly nymphs out of natural lamb's wool, flattened, and darkened on the back; they are easy to make and work as well as any on our Catskill streams. Once I allowed the wool on a nymph to loosen and bunch up—I am a wretched tier—and it emerged from the flattening press with the shape of a miniature badminton bat. For some silly reason I saved it.

Years later, I came into the upper Neversink to fish after a flood that had shifted the stones and so made it likely that stonefly nymphs would be moving about. Then I discovered that the only specimen of my nymph that I had was the sorry one I have described. I tied it on without hope but on my first cast, a strike; on my second, one of the small brook trout which there abound. Another cast, another fish; and thereafter either a fish or a strike at almost every cast. This was much too good to be true and I was mystified until at last I remembered the one banjo-shaped food organism in those streams—*Cottus,* the flat-headed, bottom-dwelling freshwater sculpin known variously as miller's-thumb, muddler, darter, and in Canada, cockatouche. It is the deadliest of trout baits but little used because it is so difficult to see and catch. Obviously, my nymph imitated a tiny muddler.

So up to the Junction Pool, reputed to harbor a great fish. Goliath, behold the master of the river! One back cast, right into the high-heaped stones behind me. End of nymph.

I suppose I've tied scores of slim-bodied lures with round, flattened heads. None was ever worth the small amount of time it took to tie it.

*   *   *

The West Branch of the Croton River, near New York City and a part of its water-supply system, incredibly is still a pretty good trout stream in spite of being terrifically hard-plugged. One early-season Saturday, long ago, I found the water at 43 degrees F. and no less than forty-eight worm fishermen in sight with not a trout among them. Entered an acquaintance of mine who dwelt close to that stream, Bob Crane, and began taking fish literally as fast as he could hook, play, and return them. To say that he soon had an audience is the height of understatement.

I elbowed my way to him and murmured, "What is it?" Bob, who wasn't above mystifying the yokelry, palmed his lure and granted me a quick look at it. On a long-shank hook he had wound a green rubber band, darkened the back with rubber cement, and tied a turn of drab hackle around its neck.

But that green was a *green* green—a Paris Green green, a cholera morbus green, a poison green: it was *green*. All I had was a bucktail lure with a bottle-green wool body. I sheared off the hair and could get strikes on that body but no fish; it wasn't green enough.

Saturday night in the Stamford, Connecticut, of that era was no time or place to buy tying materials, but I finally got a box of long-shank Carlisle saltwater hooks, a hank of wool, and sundry jars of variously green model-airplane lacquer. I made a dozen nymphs late that night and retired to dream of being king of the river. But next morning I found the water at 48 degrees and every worm fisherman with a limit of fish. No trout would look at a green nymph.

For years thereafter I never failed to try my green nymphs in that stream when the water was 43 degrees. I got some information from one of those rare fishermen you meet who knows anything about stream entomology. He assured me that there was indeed a "big green caddis" in the Croton River which he had never found in any adjacent water. This encouraged me mightily and I tried hard. But I never had so much as a strike on a green nymph.

*   *   *

I once found in Paul R. Needham's *Trout Streams* (a book which I most heartily recommend to any beginner who wants to get background on stream entomology) a reference to the *Rhyacophila* caddis, along with a photograph showing it to be a deeply segmented worm. It crawls freely on the bottom and, said the book, it is green. There was no scale in the black-and-white photograph so I had to guess at size and color. I guessed the length as one and a half inches.

That much brass "bead chain," such as is used on electric-light pulls, provided both segmentation and bottom-seeking weight. A light-wire No. 14 hook lashed to it rode point up and so avoided fouling on the stones. My lacquer jars provided a *green* green.

It cast horribly, even with a bass-bug rod, but it *would* go to the bottom even in a fast, deep run. I picked a run about four feet deep and with an even, steady current—opposite the old Swiss-American; it had a reputation then for big fish—and made it my laboratory. In the first two weeks of July, and then only, I caught a succession of the most amazingly huge chub, pot-bellied aldermen, round as rolling pins and longer. Eventually I lost all three nymphs, all in the same way; as the line tightened and the nymph started up from the streambed I would sustain a tremendous strike that cleaned me off.

For years afterward I made and tried innumerable bead-chain nymphs and couldn't get even a chub with them in that or any other run. I also discovered that *Rhyacophila* is perhaps a quarter-inch long and very, very dark green. So I don't even know what I was imitating. But why did only those three nymphs work?

So there is the lot, and you can have them. Long cogitation convinces me that, after all, it would really be very boring to be master of the river.

*   *   *

There are still things about fish and wild animals that no one seems able to explain, mysterious phenomena which doubtless are manifestations of the instinct of self-preservation. How, for instance, do all the fish in a pool learn, almost as soon as you have caught one or two of them, that your of-fering is dangerous? What makes a big trout gradually aware of your unmoving presence? Why does an animal which is quite unalarmed when first encountering you at close range finally become frightened even though you have not so much as winked?

In the days when Ed Hewitt stocked his water on the Never-sink with hundreds of "big fish"—trout of two to six pounds—it was his custom to catch out as many as he could at the end of the season, and winter them in his rearing pools, safe from the destructive Neversink floods. We whom he used to invite to help him used heavy rods, strong leaders, and bait; and we horsed our fish out and into the carrying cans as quickly as possible so as not to exhaust them with long play.

At that season the fish would be congregated in the pools below the undercut dams with which Ed had improved his stream. He would chum each of these holes in turn with a handful of the same food he had fed all season to keep these big fish in condition. This was "sheep plucks and pig melts" or, in plain language, slaughterhouse offal. The fish always went for these bloody gobbets like sharks. When they had cleaned up the offering we'd bait a big hook with a nice chunk, toss in another handful of chum, and drop the baited hook in the middle of it.

For the most part, the fish would clean up the chum like kids at a cookie jar and leave the baited hook untouched. Only when we cast carefully so as to give the bait a free natural float, or rather swim, was there a chance of hooking a fish. That can be explained; they noticed the unnatural mo-tion of a bait dragging in the current. But the curious thing was this: On the first try we'd get three or four fish out of maybe twenty. On the second we'd likely get one. On the

third and subsequent tries we'd probably get none. A few
hours later we could go back and do the same thing again;
but no amount of fishing would get all, or nearly, all of them.

Another instance: Years ago the state of Kansas made some
interesting experiments with raising black bass for stocking,
a thing previously impractical since these fish demand natural,
living food. The fish culturists succeeded in raising some bass
to fair size by cultivating daphnia—water fleas—in a series of
ponds and turning the fish into each pond in rotation, allowing the crop to replenish itself meanwhile in the other ponds.
They even developed a dry food that the fish would eat.

The trouble came when they tried to get the fish out of the
ponds to stock elsewhere. Weeds and obstructions made netting impracticable, and in those days the electric shocker
hadn't been invented. It was finally decided that the only
way to get any bass at all was by catching them, one at a
time, on hook and line.

But even that was not nearly good enough. Although the
fishermen could stick a cube of the dry food on a hook and get
good results at first, the fish quickly became warier and warier
until none could be caught, although the pond was still
crawling with them. Furthermore, they built up a residual
suspicion; resting the pond would improve the fishing after
the first try, but the improvement was less each time until
soon further fishing wasn't worth the infinitesimal results it
produced.

In the cases of both the Neversink trout and the Kansas
bass, note well that every fish that bit was derricked quickly
and quietly out of the water and into the carrying can. No
fish were hooked and lost; there was no chance of an escaped fish "telling the others," as we firmly believed when I
was a boy. Furthermore, fish are always darting around at

feeding time, and one that finds a mouthful takes off swiftly so that the others won't steal it—actions just like those of a hooked fish. How, then, can the Word pass so quickly among the fish, not only that there is danger where the fisherman is operating but that something normally good to eat is now the proximate cause of danger?

Trout fishermen with long memories can recall the rise and fall in popularity of quite a few flies. The Quill Gordon, the fanwing Royal Coachman, the long-hackled variant, and the longer-hackled spider, the Ratface Macdougal, with a unique body composed of the bristling ends of deer hair, the parachute fly with its hackle horizontal on its back instead of vertical around its neck, the Bivisible hackled from end to end with a white "indicator" for the front face, even George LaBranche's once-famous Pink Lady, each had its turn at being the irresistible, surefire, creel-filling wonder. And after this success had set every angler on the stream to using it, each in its turn became just another fly, good on its day but no better than any other over an extended period.

The rudimentary nature of the trout's brain forbids any assumption that it can reason or even think. Is it possible, then, that its faculties are so keen and its instinct so highly developed that by merely seeing the artificial often enough, it can discern the difference between a clipped deer-hair body and the legs of a natural caterpillar, a distinction it was incapable of making a year or even a month earlier? It seems hard to believe, harder yet when we consider that once the lure has lost its vogue and gone largely out of use, it never regains its original deadliness, not even years later when there probably isn't a fish in the stream old enough to have been there during the original slaughter.

*   *   *

The reaction of many creatures in the presence of a human being who "freezes" into immobility can be explained in only one way—that they can feel the weight of the human eye. This is seemingly impossible and yet I believe it implicitly simply because there seems to be no other explanation. It is the more perplexing because all creatures do not react in the same way. For instance, when I float down a winding stream, motionless in a canoe, the current will take me quite close to black or canvasback ducks, muskrats, and various other small creatures before they take alarm; but the instant I come around a bend into the sight of mud turtles sunning themselves on snag or mudbank, there is a hasty mass dive of all the turtles in sight, even though I have not flicked an eyelash.

On the other hand, it is not too uncommon for the angler who has been standing motionless in the stream for some time (in my own case, I am usually working a tangle out of a fine leader) to glance up and find himself face to face with a big fish, maybe no more than ten feet away. I mean a *big* fish, a trout of three to five pounds or even more, one of the wariest creatures that exist. Seldom can one tell where such a monster came from, but whether he drifted down with the current or swam slowly up against it, you may be positive that he is not alarmed or uneasy, for otherwise he simply wouldn't be there.

The angler was, of course, motionless before the fish appeared, and he now becomes, so to speak, twice as motionless while he tries to figure out a way to offer a fly to this leviathan without making an alarming motion. Notwithstanding that he remains as motionless as a bronze statue, he will soon see the fish become uneasy and depart. Like a boy or a dog unexpectedly in proximity to a feared enemy, the fish may try to move nonchalantly, as if he had not seen the danger, and retreat without turning his back. But boy, dog, or big fish, as soon as enough distance has been gained, will execute a lightning-fast turn and then flee with his throttle right on the floorboards.

I recall once standing straddle on two stones, casting up into broken water on Turkey Hollow Brook, a little ledge-bottomed stream that held a few enormous trout and nothing else. My fly drowned and I made a slight roll-casting motion to bring it to the surface; then a huge shape like a cruising submarine came out from under the broken water, following the fly I had picked off the water an instant before.

I froze, and the fish did just what I expected. He was too big and smart to turn and fight his way back against the current in order to regain his station; he kept coming downstream, swam between my feet, turned in the slack water behind my left foot and went back deliberately upstream in the eddy alongside the current, back into the broken water out of which he had come. I had a most excellent look at him; if he wasn't two feet long I am a minnow—and I'm no minnow.

I had just lighted a full pipe and now I stood on those stones utterly motionless until I had smoked it down to the ultimate ash. Then, an inch at a time, I drew in the fly, dried it on my shirt, and with a tiny sidewise flick of the low-held rod, threw it again up onto the broken water.

I had my trouble for my pains, just as I had known I would. When that fish went back into the shelter of the riffle, he kept right on going back to his personal hideout, and I doubt if he fed again that day; big fish are like that.

Now, that fish had not been alarmed or even uneasy when he swam between my feet or he never—repeat, never—would have done such a thing. His movements back upstream were leisurely and assured; doubtless he had often used exactly that maneuver to take food that had been carried past him by the current. I know that no movement of mine could have alarmed him, not even my cautious cast—hadn't I been casting over him for ten minutes before he came down the current after my fly? Then why did he take off? I can only think that on his way back to his station he felt my burning gaze. Probably he didn't instantly recognize what the danger was, but he didn't need to; when in doubt a big fish goes away.

I've had the same thing happen with animals. My strangest experience came one late afternoon as I stood in the backwater at the head of the Big Bend Pool on Hewitt's Neversink. As I glanced up after a long effort to untangle a fine leader, I saw a piece of driftwood floating awash right in front of me, so close I could have touched it with the tip of my nine-foot rod. In a vague way it surprised me; there had been nothing in the backwater when I was casting, so this bit of wood must have come down the current to the end of that long pool and slowly back up the countercurrent of the eddy; I must have spent a long time on that leader, I meditated. Then I saw the driftwood start moving upstream and recognized it for the back of a half-grown beaver. There were several beaver colonies on Hewitt's stretch then, and at that season the young were striking out for themselves.

Three times that beaver swam back and forth within ten feet of me, looking me over with beady, suspicious eyes, before he decided that I was just another stump. Then he went to some alders that grew below me at the water's edge, cut down a stem, dragged it into the shallow water, and began feeding on the tender bark. As I watched him I noticed that the shadow of a bare, dead tree on the horizon lay across the sand just to the water's edge, and realized that it was near sunset.

Now, I know that up to this time the beaver had felt perfectly secure, for I cannot believe that otherwise he would have gone about the business of getting a meal within twenty feet of me. But soon, evidently, he began to feel uneasy, for he turned the branch in the water until it was pointing at me and he was more or less hidden as he gnawed away at the butt end.

It was weary standing, but I was too enthralled to risk the slightest movement. The shadow of the skyline tree moved with infinite slowness across the Big Bend and finally touched the precipitous, rocky bank. As it lay on the white sand bottom beneath that crystal water, it seemed a shadow path a foot wide.

The instant—the very instant—the shadow touched the far bank, the beaver dived noiselessly and without a ripple, swam across the stream *exactly in that shadow path,* and disappeared into the ten-foot depth of blue green water against the far bank! It seemed obvious to me that he had waited for some sort of cover so that he wouldn't have to cross in silhouette against a sunlit, brilliant sand bottom, in such dangerous proximity to an enemy.

I have no idea how long I watched that beaver; it must have been an hour at least. I was so stiff I nearly toppled into the stream when I took my first step; my neck ached, my eyes burned, the tobacco in my pipe was a sodden dottle, and the leader in my hand was bone-dry. But I think that any outdoorsman who reads this will understand how light my heart was as I took the path for home.

THE ANGLER BREECHED

A LADY'S NIGHTGOWN MAY BE ROMANTIC, BUT A GENTLEMAN'S pajamas are merely ludicrous. That is the best example I can cite of the curious fact that some garments are inherently comical while others of the same general sort are not. Thus, the fisherman's battered hat is merely disreputable; his coat of many pockets, incomprehensible; and his heavy brogans, functional. But his waders are just plain ridiculous. There are waders which are more or less sightly because they have been custom-cut with such skill that every surface and seam is shaped to the contours of the wearer, but most waders are a matter of straight lines and plenty of slack, having been hewn out rather than cut, and they cannot help but excite the mirth of any observer who is not a fisherman.

The history of waders reflects the public's lack of regard for them. In the days of the brook trout, the rubber boot sufficed to wade the small cold streams in which the square-tail lurked. The rubber boot was something a farmer could understand; he had a pair himself. But who in the world could conceive of a pair of rubber pants with feet in them, like children's nightdrawers—who but an Englishman! So the first and for many years the only waders in this country were imported from England by a handful of wealthy, sophisticated city anglers. Small wonder that in the old days a fisherman in waders was such an astonishing and mirth-provoking sight that spectators haw-hawed loudly and crowds of small boys sat by the hour on bridge or bank waiting for the dude to fall in. When Fred White chose "O. U. Waders" for one of his noms de plume in *The Anglers' Club Bulletin* he was but harking back to a time when every urchin greeted him with that paraphrase of the then-popular "Oh, you kid."

Further evidence appears in a line of calendar art that has been published for generations, the work of a father and son each named Henry Hintermeister. The characters in all the paintings are largely the same: The hero is a sort of angling Richard Harding Davis, ruddy, handsome, and with a hearty enjoyment of his friends' troubles; he wears a high white collar and smokes a cigar. Members of the supporting cast are all dressed more or less alike in old business clothes. Then there are the local characters—small boy, farmer, constable. And there is the butt of every scene, the comical chap, the fall guy—short, fat, clumsy, perspiring, and always in trouble. He is the one who buys the country boy's trout, is caught poaching by the sheriff, and falls in while his friends laugh. And he is the only one in any of the pictures who wears waders; the other fishermen are all equipped with manly American rubber boots.

Besides being ridiculous, waders are treacherous, demanding, aggravating, uncomfortable, troublesome, and expensive, and I have small regard for them. However, I must make an exception for one pair that had quite a history. One day my wife came across an apparently brand-new pair of English waders in one of those junk stores called thrift shops.

"What are those?" demanded the deceitful minx, who at that moment had a pair of custom-cut Cordings of her own.

"I don't know; something for fishing," replied the volunteer clerk.

"My husband fishes. . . . How much are they?"

"Two dollars."

"Oh, that's too much," exclaimed my wife, who comes from New England. "I'll give you a dollar."

The waders had belonged, I found later, to a local man of means who had outfitted for salmon, tried it once, and given it up. As my wife had shrewdly surmised, the waders fitted me, and I wore them for two years. Then World War II came along and a young friend of mine, Ray Dierks, became a ski trooper and went to training camp in Colorado, where he found fishing. He wrote to me for flies and leaders, and lamented his lack of waders in the cold water, so I shipped him the dollar waders to wear inside his GI shoes, and he had a lot of fun until one day he encountered the colonel.

"Waders!" exclaimed the brass in pleased surprise. *"I wonder if they'd fit me?"*

So poor Ray was ranked out of his waders; but the colonel was a sport and used them only half the time, and he had a jeep with which they fished farther and better waters, so it came out about even. When Ray was transferred, the waders came back to me, but the next spring I got word that Scotty Conover, who came up from Virginia each year for a month on the Beaverkill, was marooned at the Brooklyn Flyfishers by the disintegration of his waders. Once more the dollar waders went forth and provided a good fellow with sport.

They came back but not to stay. More men than I can recall borrowed them in such rapid succession that they never had a chance to cool off. Then the war ended and I got my waders back. And they still had some two years' wear in them before they came to their end like the One Hoss Shay, all at once, when I slipped, made a long stretch, and split them from belt to ankle. It was the best buck my wife ever spent.

When I said that most waders do not have the shape of a man, I do not mean that they cannot be mistaken for one. In fact, I have in mind two instances of just that thing happening. In the first, my friend Eddie and I were coming home from fishing on a motorcycle in the sidecar of which I had a pair of navy submarine-type waders—boot feet, with a pair of blue mackintosh trousers, which were worn outside them. (Don't ask me why; that's the way I got them from the surplus store.) As we dropped down the Monticello Hill, an oncoming car broke out of line and ran into us, ditching the motorcycle and sending Eddie and me flying over the handlebars. People came running, not to us but to the overturned sidecar.

"My God, there's a man under there!" exclaimed the first to arrive.

That was news to me, and I walked over groggily to look. It certainly seemed like it, for those trousered waders, the legs horribly twisted as if the bones in them had been shattered, protruded from beneath the sidecar. It embarrassed me to tell the onlookers the truth, and somehow they seemed a bit indignant at having been deceived.

The other instance was told to me by a plumber who declared it had given him the worst scare of his life. He had

been summoned by telephone to go up into the organ loft
of a church to make some repairs. Imagine his feelings when,
as he mounted the stairs, the first thing he saw by the eerie
light of one dim bulb was the feet and legs of a man dangling
six inches above the floor.

"I thought the dominie had hung himself," he confessed,
but it was just a pair of boot-foot waders. Incidentally, it may
be useful to remember that some Baptist clergymen use waders
professionally. When waders disappeared from tackle stores
during the last war, Dana Lamb, one of my more resourceful
friends, obtained a splendid pair of boot-foot Hodgmans, in
a neat clerical black, by canvassing the religious supply houses
on Barclay Street, New York.

A few of our tribulations with waders arise from our own
lack of judgment, and this is particularly so in the matter of
filling waders with water to test them for leaks. Anyone who
tries it will quickly discover that not only does water weigh
sixty-four pounds to the cubic foot but it is completely limp
unless frozen. A pair of waders full of water weighs twice as
much as an ordinary man can lift and is as difficult to handle
as an armful of tapioca pudding.

The only time I tried it I used considerable forethought
although not nearly enough. I put a sawhorse beside the basement laundry tubs so I could use the hose to fill the waders,
which were set astride the sawhorse. And I put hooks in the
ceiling from which cords ran to the suspender buttons to hold
the waders upright. It worked like a charm. In no time at all I
was able to mark the leaks in this "man" who sat so firmly
astride his wooden horse and looked so much like me when
I neglect my diet. Then I emptied the waders.

Who has not looked back at some catastrophe and shuddered at the stupidity and mental blindness that drove him into it? My silly solution of the problem was to loosen the cords while I held the man upright, and then pick him up and empty him into the tubs!

Who was that wretched creature that crept like a drowned rat up the basement stairs to evoke the remonstrances of his wife and the mirth of his offspring? And who labored for a week to get the dampness out of the cellar while his tools rusted merrily on the workbench? Who but the author!

The water test is a handy one, but the way to use it is to fill only one leg of the waders and check it, then turn the water into the other leg, and finally into the seat. Even so, it's a two-man job.

The worst of the long list of wader woes that I ever heard of happened not to me but to an able and devoted angler, C. Otto von Kienbusch. Under the title "A Tale of Woe," I wrote the story of it in *The Anglers' Club Bulletin* as follows:

Like the mayfly, Otto spends eleven months of the year in a stone-bound crevice at the bottom of the stream which is New York City, dreaming of his springtime metamorphosis. But when June comes he rises to the surface, casts off his nymphal shuck, and then on shining gauzy wings flies off to Canada for a month of dry-fly salmon fishing on his miles of the Patapedia. Just as the mayfly cannot eat after its metamorphosis, so the angler cannot buy tackle once he has spread his wings, so all must be in order beforehand—and if you know Otto, you know it is.

Last winter, that his wings might be even shinier and his flight stronger, Otto decided to fit himself with those expensive, magnificently custom-tailored waders that take four months to get from England and are worth it. With thoughts of all the future Junes on the Patapedia, he bought the apotheosis of all waders, the extra-heavy kind guaranteed for ten years.

June approached and Otto began to stir about the stream bottom and make his last preparations for flight. All must be anticipated, all made perfect. Judge then of his consternation when one suspender button on the waders was discovered to be ever so slightly loose. A lackey bore them to the tailor. Time passed. The battery of new rods, the jeweled reels, the freshly imported lines, the gaudy flies, the tons of gadgets were ready—all but the waders that would make their use possible. Finally, a week before departure time, they came and Otto unpacked them.

Bessie McCoy might have sung "The Yama Yama Man" in them, those faintly indecent drawers. The Fisk Rubber "Time to Re-Tire" boy in his childish nightdrawers, now presumably grown to manhood, might have been at home in them. Adorned with ribbons, they might have set a new style in undies. But Otto will never, never cast the light fly to the silver salmon in them, for the tailor had had them dry-cleaned, thus removing every vestige of rubber from their fabric. And then had pressed them in neat creases.

FANTASIA

WHEN YOU HAVE FISHED A RIVER AS LONG AS I HAVE FISHED
the Beaverkill, you will have a great stock of memories connected with it and eventually find it difficult sometimes to
recall which are fact and which fantasy. Just as the water of
the famed Hassayampa renders those who drink of it incapable
of telling the truth, so the water of the Beaverkill renders
those who have soaked their legs in it too long incapable of
separating actuality from fancy. So although the event which
I shall relate did indeed happen on the Little River, I cannot
now tell whether it occurred in fact or only in my imagination.

It was one of those hot, drowsy August midafternoons when
there is no possibility of taking a trout because they have all
fled from such tepid waters, and the angler has an opportunity
to practice fancy casting without the risk of being surprised by
a strike. It was a day for smoking a pipe and idling in the
river instead of concentrating on the industrious pursuit of

the prey, and a perfect time for diffuse meditation of the most worthless and unproductive sort.

So eventually I fell to pondering on the innumerable items constituting the elaborate equipment which some anglers load on their shoulders and in their pockets in an effort to make up for their inability to perform the basic operation of fishing—finding a fish. I was idly trying to calculate how many accessories an angler really could carry when a clangor assailed my ears. Surely that noise downstream was a truckload of steel rails passing over a cobbled street; and yet I knew there was no road so close to the river. The noise grew louder and then its source was revealed. Around the bend staggered a startling apparition, an upright object on legs. As I watched, it collapsed with a clang of smitten metal.

When I reached the thing, I found that its head was a metal protuberance with a glass plate in front through which I could see the face of a man, drawn and blue, apparently from strangulation. The thing was human! Indeed, it was a fisherman, for closer inspection revealed that it wore waders and a fishing coat beneath an almost complete covering composed of an infinite variety of small objects. With a sharp twist I unscrewed the globular helmet.

"What in the world is this?" I muttered as I regarded the strange contraption. The man's eyes opened, and his expression changed from distress to pride.

"Head net—combination fly net and diving helmet," he gasped. His strength began to return, and he sat up with a crash. Fumbling among the objects which covered him, he brought forth a flat metal case.

"Join me?" he invited. I looked my question.

"Patent siphon-flask," he explained, pride in his voice.

"Ready-mixed highballs, all carbonated." He fizzed a drink into a folding cup, downed it, and brightened up.

"Sorry this happened," he apologized, proffering a case which dispensed cigarettes already lighted. "Guess I tried to cover too much ground," and he indicated a farmhouse several hundred yards away as his starting point. I now realized that I had met a gadget carrier, and in order to head off the detailed exhibition and demonstration of his whole equipment which I knew inevitably would be forthcoming, I moved to depart.

"Nice to have met you, Mr. . . ."

"Abercrombie Mills Hardy," he replied, drawing out a card case. At that instant a chub struck at my trailing fly and began to make merry in the pool.

"I'll net him for you!" shrieked Abercrombie, aiming a short aluminum tube and pressing a button. A collapsible arm shot out some twenty feet, there was a loud snap, and the chub was imprisoned in a sort of self-closing frame covered with netting. Abercrombie chortled triumphantly. It took us nearly half an hour to get the fish out of the net, and we had just freed him when a fish rose above us.

"Your fish; put a fly over him," I suggested.

"Sorry, I can't," said Abercrombie regretfully. "Left my rod at the farmhouse."

"You forgot your *rod?*" I exclaimed incredulously.

"No, I didn't forget it," he said. "You see, I have so much to carry . . ."

Ah, well, let him without sin cast the first hook-sharpening stone. I cannot, for my fishing vest weighs precisely five pounds.

THE MEDICAL ASPECTS
OF ANGLING

ANGLING LITERATURE IS FULL OF TESTIMONIALS TO THE THERapeutic value of angling. Most of the testifiers have kept their statements safely general, but a few have not hesitated to go out on a limb by giving particulars. When the present writer happened to read two of them in succession, he was moved to quote them as horrible examples of how a fisherman can tamper with the truth when his enthusiasm carries him away.

The first is from *Hints on Angling*, by a writer who protected himself with the pseudonym "Palmer Hackle Esq.," published in 1846. He relates how fishing saved a man from, of all things, strong drink:

"But angling is not only a most agreeable and delightful amusement—it also imparts health and long life to its zealous and devoted disciples. We have witnessed its powerfully healing virtues, even at the very gates of death itself. When we have seen a poor wretch abandon himself to the habits of unmitigated intemperance—when he has thrown off every feeling of decency and decorum—when we have perceived the reddened eye, the blotched face, the trembling hand, the tottering step, the dull and idiotic air; when he has endured repeated attacks of 'delirium tremens,' and his liver has become enlarged and as hard as a Norfolk dumpling—when he has shivered all over with palsy, and his very bowels become feculent with disease—when he has had a hard dry cough, one that comes by fits and seems to tear his emaciated carcase to pieces—when his breath has been like the effluvium of a jakes, or the exhalations of a rotten fen—when rising from his frowsy and restless bed, he has not been able to swallow a single mouthful, nor to carry that mouthful to his head, without previously drenching his stomach with bitters and brandy—when dry colic and offensive diarrhea have taken turn and turn about on his miserable intestines—when his legs have swelled as big as mill-posts, and surcharged with water—when tapping has grown useless by repetition and belladonna has ceased to act—when his chest has been as full of bilge water as the wreck of a leaky herring smack—when, in fact, he has become one incarnation of filth and disease, we have taken him by the hand, led him quietly to the banks of some pleasant stream and put a rod in his languid grasp; and then, with the indispensable assistance of Father Mathew, have restored him with renovated health to his heart-broken family, and again made him a useful member of society."

The Reverend William H. H. Murray, pastor of a socially elevated Boston church—who lost his pulpit through a fondness for racehorses, went to the then-desperate frontier of Texas to run what was called, probably euphemistically, a restaurant, and returned to become a minister again and finally die in bed—was a huge, vigorous, he-man type who wrote several books on the joys of the out-of-doors. In one of them, *Adventures in the Wilderness, or Camp Life in the Adirondacks,* published in 1869, he told a tale which sent so many consumptives to their doom in the Adirondack forests that he earned condemnatory editorials in the New York newspapers.

"I recall," he wrote, "a young man, the son of wealthy parents in New York, who lay dying in that great city, attended as he was by the best skill that money could secure. A friend calling upon him one day chanced to speak of the Adirondacks, and that many had found help from a trip to their region. From that moment he pined for the woods. He insisted on what his family called his insane idea that the mountain air and the aroma of the forest would cure him. It was his daily request and entreaty that he might go. At last his parents consented, the more readily because the physicians assured them that their son's recovery was impossible and his death a mere matter of time.

"They started with him for the north in search of life. When he arrived at the point where he was to meet his guide, he was too reduced to walk. The guide, seeing his condition, refused to take him into the woods, fearing, as he plainly expressed it, that he would die on his hands. At last another guide was prevailed upon to serve him, not so much for the money, as he afterward told me, but because he pitied the young man and felt that one so near death as he was should be gratified even in his whims.

"The boat was half filled with cedar, pine, and balsam boughs, and the young man, carried in the arms of his guide from the house, was laid full length upon them. The camp utensils were put at one end, and the guide seated himself at the other, and the little boat passed with the living and the dying down the lake, and was lost to the group watching them among the islands to the south. This was early June.

"The first week, the guide carried the young man on his back over all the portages, lifting him in and out of the boat as he might a child. But the healing properties of the balsam and pine, which were his bed by day and night, began to exert their power. Awake or asleep, he inhaled their fragrance. Their pungent and healing odors penetrated his diseased and irritated lungs. The second day out his cough was less sharp and painful. At the end of the first week he could walk by leaning on the paddle. The second week he needed no support. The third week the cough ceased entirely. From that time he improved with wonderful rapidity.

"He 'went in' the first of June, carried in the arms of his guide. The second week of November he 'came out' bronzed as an Indian, and as hearty. In the five months he had gained sixty-five pounds of flesh, and flesh, too, 'well packed on,' as they say in the woods. Coming out he carried the boat over all portages; the very same over which a few months before the guide had carried him, and pulled as strong an oar as any amateur in the wilderness. His meeting with his family I leave to the reader to imagine. The wilderness received him almost a corpse. It returned him to his home and the world as happy and healthy a man as ever bivouacked under its pines."

Fishing, anybody? How about a spot of camping?

RAIN ON THE BRODHEAD

BRODHEAD'S CREEK IS CALLED, BY THOSE WHO LOVE THIS beautiful stream with constancy unalterable, "the biggest little river," meaning that it provides fine fishing out of all proportion to its size. But one who goes on it after being used to the shallow Catskill streams will quickly add another meaning because he will discover that for its size it contains a surprising amount of water.

The typical Catskill river has its depth in the middle, with thin edges and a stony foreshore which is kept clear by the roaring floods that afflict those streams. Only where there is an occasional short stretch of steep, rocky bank can a tree overhang the water or offer its roots to the trout for a refuge. Not so the Brodhead. It too is a lively, tumbling river, but its high, square-cut banks are thick with trees and brush, the roots of which are almost continuous along the streamside. Here the greatest depth is frequently right next the banks, which are usually undercut, providing the trout with a kind of cover of which the Catskill streams are almost devoid.

As Dick Hunt's guest I have fished both the Parkside Angling Association and the Brodhead Fly Fishers' Club water a number of times, but one in particular remains in my memory as a fishless day. Now Dick cannot be called an expert because he claims that there are none, but only "knowledgeable" fishermen; but it is surprising how many "knowledgeable" salmon anglers say he is the best low-water salmon fisherman in America, and how many "knowledgeable" trout anglers say that no one can fish a long flat as he can. This being so, and on such splendid water as the Brodhead, you might imagine that Dick and I had good insurance against a fishless day, but that would be only because you do not know me. For not only can I exorcise fish like a witch doctor and create deluges like an Indian rainmaker but I shed such an aura of ill luck that it envelops my companions as well as me.

When we arrived at the boarding house that morning, Dick unpacked certain articles with which this account deals. One was a brand-new nylon fishing raincoat so fine and thin it could be carried in any pocket, and another was a brand-new fishing vest, the outstanding feature of which was a back pocket with a vertical, zipper-closed entrance on either side, behind the wearer's elbows. Dick, who is apt to be as casual in his fishing appointments as was his friend Skues, displayed these articles with boyish pride and hearty admiration for his own foresight. The third article was a flat traveling case, familiar to all his fishing friends, holding two metal half-gallon containers, one full of whisky and the other of martinis.

I must digress here to say that there are two things remarkable about Dick's martinis. The first is their excellence. Ostensibly the dry martini is the simplest thing in the world to make, but in fact it is of a mysterious and esoteric nature. Dick's are made of eight parts of the right gin and one part of the right vermouth; and nothing else. When I try this formula, all I get is an explosive mixture. But by some alchemy, Dick produces a drink with the spicy fragrance of an old-fashioned garden and the tinkling grace of a minuet played on the harpsichord, the most gorgeous firewater that ever charmed the palate and seduced the senses. The other remarkable thing about them is that they have to be earned. We have never set out for the stream without his reminding me that we must earn our drinks by diligent angling and the demonstration of our knowledgeability before we can have them on our return.

This day we set out for the best pool with the most incongruous name of any on the Brodhead. It is famous as Mary's Flat, and I have never ceased to protest that the name brings to mind nothing but an old musical comedy, *Up in Mabel's Room*. No city boy of my generation can think of a "flat" as anything but an apartment.

The trouble with the river was that there had been a rainy week and the Flat, which normally is pants-pocket deep, was belt-buckle deep and more, next to the bank. Furthermore, the season was between the two big Brodhead hatches and the fish were cruising, and rising only sporadically. Finally, they were cruising either along my own bank, to which I could not cast because of the overhanging verdure, or along the opposite bank—and the river was too deep to wade within casting range.

Besides all that, it was wartime and new waders were not to be had. I had had to trust to the ancient Cordings, and my first step into Mary's Flat told me that my confidence had been misplaced. As I clung to the bushes with one hand and

roll-cast a stonefly nymph across the current with the other,
I could feel icy water descending from a leak in my seat to
meet icy water rising through a leak in my left heel.

Dick was fishing dry in rather shallower water above me,
and as I fished down the current I kept turning to see if he
was getting any action. He changed flies three or four times
and then hit the right one—No. 16 Red Fox. All I could see
was the easy, pushing motion of the rod as he fished a long
and beautiful cast in under the branches on the far bank.
Then suddenly I saw a dramatic picture that sometimes returns to me in dreams. A thin white streak flashed across the
water as he whipped his line off the surface, and in the same
instant, white foam surged under the far bank as he struck
his fish.

He held his bowed rod high overhead as he reeled in his
slack, and then settled to playing the fish—it was a dandy—
in the considerate manner which 4X gut demands. He finally
grasped it, killed it, and I saw him reach around and slide it
into the back pocket of his new vest. The next time I looked,
he was pocketing another fish, and pretty soon his rod arched
again to the third victim, which followed its predecessors into
his back pocket.

It was while I was watching him take off and kill his fourth
fish (he wanted to take some home to a friend) that I got
what could only be called a bite on my trailing nymph—a
savage strike that straightened out my arm and then broke
the leader. I was as far downstream as I could wade, so I
turned to watch Dick while I soaked another leader point.
Imagine my astonishment at seeing the usually staid and
sober Hunt striding downstream as fast as three feet of water
would permit and at every second step plunging his arm in

up to the armpit. He was a sorry sight when he finally desisted and waded to the bank, one sleeve and his shirtfront sopping, and water in the front pocket of his waders and the fly box that reposed therein.

The explanation was simple. Immediately after pocketing his fourth fish, he had been astonished to see it floating away. Only then did he discover that the other entrance to his back pocket was unzipped, and as fast as he had inserted fish at one side, they had been sliding out at the other. His race downstream had been a futile pursuit of his fourth fish.

He hoisted himself ashore with many disparaging comments on the new vest, and as he did so, the heavens split apart and released a torrent of rain like the descent of Niagara Falls. I whipped out the short raincoat and waterproof hat cover which I always carry and exhorted Dick to do the same.

"Your new raincoat is starting to pay dividends already," I said.

Dick stood still with a very curious expression on his face.

"I left it in the car," he said softly. There ensued what could only be called a pregnant silence, for the car was half a mile away.

"Ah, well," he said at last, "here is a good thick tree," and led the way to a bushy hemlock beneath which we sheltered, he soaked down to the waist and I up to the same line of demarcation. We squatted on our heels and I remarked that it was "cowboy style."

"I *was* a cowboy for three or four years. Didn't I ever tell you?" he replied, and then began one of the most absorbing recitals that I can call to mind. As I remember it, he had had no shooting scrapes or fantastic adventures, although there was one pretty thrilling near-stampede and another tense moment when he almost had been left afoot on the prairie after dismounting. But he brought the color and flavor of a cowboy's life so close that I could smell the bitter smoke of sagebrush and taste the dust that envelops the drag riders. We forgot all about the rain and our discomfort, and in those unlikely circumstances I, at least, enjoyed a half hour of fascinating discourse.

About noon the rain finally let up and we went back to the house. Wet waders and sodden clothes were never peeled off quicker, and by the time I came back downstairs, Dick was opening the traveling case.

"I think," he said judicially, "that we have earned a *good* drink."

We had a hearty lunch and then retired to the living room to plan for the afternoon. The decision was not difficult to make, for rain slashed at the windows and charged level along the ground as the gusts swept by. So we took a fishing book apiece and bade defiance to the weather in the very best kind of fishing for such a day—reading about it. But not for long; the ineffable sense of well-being that comes from being warm, dry, and replete overcame us, and we dozed the afternoon away.

*   *   *

That was long ago, of course, but the memory of this fishless day is not only clear but doubly precious to me, for Dick is no longer with us and two great storms have obliterated Mary's Flat and made the Brodhead, although still a fine fishing stream, strange water to me.

ONE LINE FROM A DIARY

SHORTLY BEFORE HIS DEATH, MY DEAR FRIEND DICK CLARK wrote me:

"Today I found a notation in my diary: 'Friday, June 16, 1961. Hawley, Pa, with Sparse.' That was the last time we fished together.

"That was the week-end we drove about, looking for a certain stream reputed to be full of big, stream-bred browns. We found it, too, but it turned out to be just a worm stream buried in brush so we could not fish it. Instead, we drove alongside it on a dirt road for a few hundred yards, with a young grouse walking calmly ahead of us until he was ready to leave the road and head for the brush alongside. Remember how we laughed at his audacity?

"We did not fish that day until after dinner, then we drove to the Dyberry to fish the 'Fly Only' water above the bridge. I started well above you in the open water and hooked into

121

a monster that took my fly and several feet of 6X leader, just as it got too dark to tie on another tippet.

"When we got back to the White Deer Inn, Joe d'Annibale laughed at us and our fishing, went into the kitchen and returned with a glass tray containing eight or ten lovely brookies which some country kid had snatched from some hidden beaver pond. My, weren't they beautiful, Sparse! We had a couple apiece for breakfast the next morning. And weren't they delicious! Remember?

"I shall always remember that trip and the simple pleasure we had, just knocking about the countryside, fishing a bit, the humor of coming back to the Inn fishless and our host grinning from ear to ear without losing his cigar butt, then bringing out those beautiful little brookies, still full of color and as shiny as when they were first taken from the beaver pond. Fishless day indeed! Who could have had a better time?"

THE QUEST FOR
THEODORE GORDON

FIRST THERE WAS THEODORE GORDON, THE CONSUMPTIVE EXILED
to the Catskills, whose cosmopolitan personality and passion
for angling enabled him to project his spirit across the ocean
into kinship with the great figures of contemporary British
angling; he was, in fact, the father of dry-fly angling in America. He died in 1915.

Then there was John McDonald, scholar, writing genius
of *Fortune* magazine, and devoted angler, who more than
thirty years later rescued Gordon from oblivion by the keenness of his discernment and the ardor of his research. His
labors culminated in 1947 in the angling literary milestone
*The Complete Fly Fisherman: The Notes and Letters of
Theodore Gordon.*

Then, some two years later, The Theodore Gordon Society (there is no connection with a conservation organization of similar name, which was formed some years later) was
formed by four members of The Anglers' Club of New York:

Lewis M. Hull (The Physicist), Guy R. Jenkins (The Underwriter), the late Edgar G. Wandless (The Attorney), and the present writer (The Reporter). Out of a chance conversation before the Club fireplace grew an expedition to the Catskills to photograph the house in which Gordon had died. On that occasion the four organized this most informal society, which eventually interviewed at length the surviving two of the three native fishermen who had been Gordon's only familiars in the Catskills, and later helped in solving the mystery of Gordon's last resting-place.

Finally, there was Virginia Kraft, then a talented writer-reporter and now an associate editor of *Sports Illustrated* magazine. In the course of authenticating Gordon's fly box for the then-new magazine, she formed a desire to know more about the man. Over the next several years she devoted several thousand miles of spare-time travel and investigation to finding and interviewing Gordon's few surviving, scattered family connections. In this manner she accumulated what meager information still was available about that little-known recluse and today undoubtedly knows more about him than any other living person. Ultimately this knowledge became the key which unlocked the mystery of Gordon's burial place.

THINGS OF THE SPIRIT

It was a most unseasonable pilgrimage for a late November weekend, a sentimental journey to find the Catskill farmhouse in which Theodore Gordon had lived his last years and died, and to see again, before a New York City reservoir should drown it, the lovely Neversink that he had fished. Unseasonable, yet it had crystallized instantly and urgently out of nowhere during a chance conversation among four angling friends. Why is not clear; but perhaps they had subconsciously in mind the news lately come from England of the death of Gordon's dear letter-friend, the great angler Skues.

They left the city that weekend in a drizzle that worsened into sleet, but they were warm and dry, and some sympathetic bond not only joined but uplifted their spirits. So while the station wagon slogged along, they sang the songs grave and gay that everyone holds in memory; and this was remarkable, for they were not a singing sort of men. Even when, at Napanoch, the sleet changed to a blinding white wall of snowflakes in the headlights and it seemed as if tire chains would be needed, they still sang, and when they came at last to Claryville, and carried their heavy lading into the frigid cabin, they sang though their teeth chattered.

Three roaring fires, a gallon of scalding coffee, and a mound of sandwiches soon made things comfortable, and they wound up smoking and chatting before the fireplace. But the first night of an expedition is nothing more, spiritually, than what the Arab caravan men call "the little start," a mere getting of the expedition on the road. So after nightcaps as tall as a cowboy's sombrero, they burrowed into heaps of five-point blankets and slept the night away.

Then it was morning, "the great start," the spiritual setting forth, with fires rekindled and the pungency of coffee summoning the sleepers to add to it the fragrance of that best smoke of the whole day, the pipe before breakfast. It was afternoon when the pilgrims finally took the road to Gordon's habitation. As the car picked its way through the deserted, ruined village of Neversink huddled amid slopes desolated by the dam builders, no reminder was needed that the shortest days of the year were at hand. The Physicist shook his head in despair as he read his light meter, and the others were depressed by the obvious approach of the day's end.

When they came to the spot, they were doubtful, for the house had been torn down, but a deer hunter who came by assured them that upon this foundation had stood the Anson Knight house, in which Gordon had lived out his last days. All this part of the valley had been condemned now for the reservoir, and the city had pulled down the dwellings at once to keep out squatters. Soon the place where Theodore Gordon had lived and died, as well as much of the river he had loved to fish, would sleep beneath a hundred feet of water.

The building site was across the road from the river and above it. A long knoll behind it was mantled with a dense windbreak of evergreens. A somber sky pressed down on the dark pines, and a pool in the river that had been bright crystal last summer now shone like black polished flint through the naked branches. The raw, wet air eddied in sullen gusts.

Sleet crunched underfoot as the pilgrims climbed the little pitch to the house and stood on the wall of a foundation filled with a mean, pathetic jumble of rubbish. Yonder still stood the rotting, unpainted barn and here were the weed-grown steps up which the weary angler must have plodded so often; but the spirit of Theodore Gordon had gone from the place and it was only a littered, dreary site.

Before they drove away, someone produced a flask and they stood together in the road looking back at the spot they had left, murmuring brief toasts to the great angler as they sipped the spirits.

"Do you suppose Gordon took a drink, on occasion?" queried The Reporter.

"I am sure that he did, but Herman Christian and others who knew him agree that he was most temperate," replied The Physicist. "In one of his later letters to Steenrod, Gordon refers to 'my bottle of whiskey which I never use' but in an earlier article he recalls a weary walk home from fishing with a companion whose flask, 'a miserable caricature of a thing,' was so small that it provided no sustenance. Theodore Gordon was gently born and reared, and lived in many places, and I think we may safely assume that he knew how to enjoy the good things of life."

It was almost dark when they got back to their cabin. A conflagration was started in the outdoor fireplace, and while it burned down to a bed of embers, The Attorney made a salad. Then, muffled to the ears, he went out to the fire with a long-handled fork in one hand and a great steak in the other. He threw the latter on the embers and a rich aroma streamed down the wind so that a benighted hunter, a hundred yards away, stopped short and then struck out for home at a quickened pace. The Reporter brought the cook a drink, and they stood together looking at the river.

"The shades of all the great anglers who knew the Neversink must still frequent this place," said The Reporter. "They must be enjoying that savory scent, right now."

" 'The gods of the place'—a pagan concept," replied The Attorney. "This steak is ready."

After dinner The Reporter went out to the woodpile, but before he carried in his load he paused to look and listen. Despite the snowy gleam of the ground, iron winter darkness lay on the land—an empty, desolate land unrelieved by even a point of light, from the peaks of Slide Mountain to the river gurgling half-frozen at his feet. But yellow lamplight streamed through the window; and inside the cozy cabin, redolent of good food and tobacco, they were singing an old college glee as they washed the dishes.

"Like a blackbird in the spring . . ." mourned the silvery tenor, the notes harmonizing sweetly.

"Oralee, Oralee, maid with golden hair," sobbed the counter tenor, and the baritone throbbed like a bronze bell. Soft and mellow, the music faded into the icy darkness, making it seem even more cold and empty. The Reporter gazed at the pool below him and imagined a frail little man casting with a nine-foot rod amid springtime greenery, placing a tiny dull-colored fly with consummate artistry. He carried in his wood, then mixed a stout drink and carried it back outdoors.

" 'The gods of the place,' " he quoted softly. "A libation to the gods of the place." He started to pour a libation in the manner of the ancients, then changed his mind and turned back to the cabin. He held the door wide and stood aside for a moment as if in invitation, then went inside and put the drink on the stone mantelshelf of the fireplace, in the shadows.

When the work was done the four sat smoking by the fire and their conversation was of Gordon, weaving into a varicolored fabric the threads of information gathered from the recollections of The Underwriter and several others of their acquaintance who had known Gordon, and from the collected letters which are almost our only record of him. They spoke of his frail physical aspect, his habit of rolling cigarettes between thumb and finger of one hand, of the mysterious "Fly Fishers" to which he several times refers in his writings as his club, and of Skues's coinage of the pen name Val Conson. It was getting late when the fire finally burned low and the room turned chilly.

"Throw on some wood," urged The Physicist with a shiver. "It's cold in here. How Gordon must have suffered, winters, in that primitive farmhouse."

"He did," affirmed The Underwriter. "It runs through his letters; he detested the cold. He was an outdoorsman, and loved the woods on a crisp, sunny winter's day, but he hated dark, raw weather like today's."

"Coldness and loneliness run through his writings," chimed in The Physicist. "Note how recurrently he says things like: 'It is too cold to work'; 'It is wild and lonely up here'; 'It is a dreary day'; 'This is a cold, raw day, damp and windy.' 'Now it is overcast, raw.' And in December 1905, he wrote in *The Fishing Gazette:* 'It is rather dreary in the country at this season. The birds have gone for the most part, the hum and buzz of insect life has ceased, the leaves, which recently were so beautiful, are on the ground, brown and withered. On a still day, Nature seems to be dead or at least in a comatose state. Even the light of day is hard and cold. As I write, the wind is shrieking and tearing at this frail wooden house as if determined to carry it off bodily.'

"The loneliness of this city-bred, cultured man imprisoned in a rude mountain settlement all winter was pathetic, and I think there was intense feeling in his remark to Skues: 'I am very lonely tonight and am writing to you for the feeling of companionship,' " concluded The Physicist.

"And now Skues is dead. What a reunion they must have had in Valhalla," mused The Reporter.

"A pagan concept," reiterated The Attorney. "It's getting late; let's turn in."

They wasted no time in their preparations for the night, but before he went to bed, The Reporter turned back to look at the glass on the mantelshelf. It was empty.

THE FRIENDS OF THEODORE GORDON

What the world knows of Theodore Gordon, the angler-epistolist, comes principally from his published letters to R. B. Marston and G. E. M. Skues in England, and the youthful Guy Jenkins; and from the recollections of his friends in the Catskills. Of these there were three; but one, Bruce Leroy, died long before without ever having recorded his impressions of Gordon. The other two were Herman Christian and Roy Steenrod, both living as this is written (1969). Herman Christian resides in Grahamsville, New York, and Roy Steenrod in his native community of Liberty, New York. Both are in retirement.

The nature of Gordon's friendship with each of his three Castkill friends differed in subtle ways. Christian and Steenrod agree that Gordon "thought a lot" of Bruce Leroy; Leroy named one of his sons after him. Yet, judging from Gordon's letters, he called him Bruce only occasionally. It is impossible to evaluate this friendship now because all we know of Leroy is that he inherited a prosperous farm at Leroy's Corners, two miles from Bradley, but preferred hunting and fishing to farming.

Herman Christian was Gordon's familiar; they lived only a quarter of a mile apart during Gordon's last years and saw a great deal of each other. Specifically, Christian fished with Gordon far more than did any other person. Gordon called him Christian, and Herman still refers to his friend as Mr. Gordon.

But Gordon never called Roy Steenrod anything but Mr. Steenrod and after ten years of correspondence still so addressed him in the salutations of his letters. Roy always refers to him as Gordon, but I think he addressed him as Mr. Gordon. Yet Roy feels that he was closer to Gordon than any of his other friends: "He told me more than anyone else in the world."

The following interviews are taken almost verbatim from my stenographic notes of a series of interviews with Herman Christian and Roy Steenrod, condensed but not altered in meaning. They are given here in the present tense, the form in which they were originally written soon after the interviews were completed in 1950 and 1955, respectively.

HERMAN CHRISTIAN

Herman Christian lives on his 176-acre farm contiguous to the Big Bend Pool of the Neversink River below Hall's Mills, so remote that the bears come into his woods to gather the juneberries (shadblow). He makes a living out of a little of everything—bees, maple syrup, timber, a small garden, trapping, hunting, fishing—"but my best crop is trout flies." At sixty-eight he carries his lean, sinewy six feet two inches erect and moves with the lithe surefootedness of the master woodsman, trapper, and hunter that he is. He gives the impression of military bearing, and one is not surprised to learn that he has been a soldier. A hawklike profile and piercing eyes give him a forbidding look, but when he smiles, his expression becomes warm and friendly.

For many years he had the reputation of being able to dance more dances, kiss more girls, and whip more men than anyone in his valley. But more than that, he is still known throughout the length and breadth of the Catskills as a peerless fisherman with the dry fly and particularly with the wet fly. Theodore Gordon himself paid tribute to his ability to find and take big fish. The following is Herman Christian's own story of his early life and his friendship with Theodore Gordon.

"I was born in Eureka, New York [in the Rondout Valley]. My father died when I was two years old. When I was fourteen I went to work on a farm near Hall's Mills [in the adjoining Neversink Valley] for three dollars a month. When I was sixteen, in 1898, I lied like hell and enlisted in the regular U.S. Army. I was assigned to the Tenth Infantry and with that organization served a year in Cuba and three years in the Philippines. Afterward I returned to the Neversink Valley. Later I became a guard at Great Meadows [New York] Prison and through an advertisement in *Field & Stream* magazine became manager of the fly-tying department of the Pflueger Tackle people in Akron.

"I was a fisherman from boyhood; fished the Neversink the first time when I was nine years old. I came with two men and we camped alongside the pool above the Big Bend. I never dreamed that I would own it sometime, but it was a part of the farm I bought thirty-three years ago. I subsequently sold the river frontage to Ed Hewitt.

"In 1896, the year I went to work on the farm, I caught my first brown trout on a line I had set for eels. He was nineteen and a half inches long and weighed two and a half pounds; I sold him for fifty cents.

"I do not recall when I began fishing with flies; I know I was using them in 1897 or 1898. Around 1906 I wanted to get Theodore Gordon to tie some flies for me—in those days he was generous in giving his flies to fishermen he knew. I asked Bruce Leroy about it, and he said that Gordon did not give flies to everybody, and suggested that I get some good feathers for him. I got some blues and gingers and took them to Mr. Gordon, and we became acquainted.

"He called me Christian. When he moved from the hotel in Neversink Village to Anson Knight's [near the Neversink Bridge; Gordon died there], they did not deliver his mail to him, and I used to bring it to him every day—I lived on the other side of the bridge, about a quarter of a mile from Knight's. He would receive ten or twelve letters a day. Mr. Gordon used to come and see me often. He went out very little in winter, but if he went out at all he would come to my house. He wanted to board with us, but I had two little girls, two and four years old, and my wife didn't want him because he had TB and had the habit of spitting on the floor when he was tying flies.

"I used to go up and talk to him a couple of hours at a time, two or three times a week. 'Gosh, Christian,' he would say, 'I'm glad you came up. It got lonesome here.' Sometimes he would give me a drink. He never drank much, but he always had a bottle of cognac or something to give a drink to anyone who came in. But when I was fishing with him I never smelt liquor on his breath.

"Whenever I located a nice big fish, the next day I'd take Mr. Gordon down to fish for it. I wouldn't take a rod myself; I'd ten times rather see him catch it. But almost always he would insist on my fishing a little with his rod while he rested. He would not fish at all, no matter how many fish rose, until the fish he wanted began to feed. When he got him, he would usually stop fishing. He never kept more than three or four fish but always good ones. He liked to give a brace of fish, or a brace of partridge or woodcock, to the Smiths who had a summer home nearby. I think Mr. Smith was a customs appraiser—they were not local people. In all my experience with Mr. Gordon, he would never fish more than a couple of pools in an afternoon, usually only one. If he could not get the one fish he had gone for, he would not care to fish any more.

"Ed Payne made Gordon a rod about 1895; Gordon tied him thirty-nine dozen flies to pay for it. About 1912, when he was staying at DeMund's Hotel in Neversink, I took him down some feathers and he went in and got this rod and said, 'I don't know anybody who would appreciate it as much as you would,' and gave it to me. I still have it and occasionally use it. It is nine and a half feet, three pieces, and of course soft, wet-fly action. [This rod is now in the collection of The Anglers' Club of New York.]

"As time went on and his illness became worse and worse, he fished closer to home, and less. The winter and spring before he died, he was so sick that he did not tie me one single fly.

"Leroy said somebody ought to get hold of Gordon's relatives and tell them of his condition; he said Gordon had a cousin living in Newburgh, New York. I started writing letters, and it took me to Haverstraw, New York, and finally to East Orange, New Jersey. I finally turned up a cousin and talked to him on the telephone, and he came up and I went to Anson Knight's with him.

"Mr. Gordon was in bed. He got up and dressed and said to his cousin sharply, 'What did you come up here for?' His cousin sort of passed it off. We visited for a while and then came back to my house, and then I took him to the train. Mr. Gordon died five or six days later.

"Theodore Gordon as I knew him did not weigh much over ninety pounds and was maybe five feet two or three inches. He was a hell of a good shot and had keen sight and hearing, but he could not tell the direction the sound came from when a bird got up behind him. He liked to get some exercise, but he could not take much owing to his health. He was a man's man in every way.

"He used to use the bamboo tip-case of his Payne rod for a walking stick. He did not need a stick, but he would take it and go strutting down to see the Smiths." (This tip case was of whole bamboo, hollowed out and fitted with a brass screw cap. For a nine-and-a-half-foot, three-piece rod it would have to be thirty-nine inches long, or considerably too long for a man of five feet two inches. The rule is, two inches added to half the user's height; a total of thirty-three inches in this case. Furthermore, the tip case now with the rod shows no sign at all of having been used as a walking stick. Since it is scarcely possible that Christian invented this little sidelight, apparently Gordon carried the case as a swagger stick, under his arm.)

"He smoked one cigarette after another—rolled them between his thumb and one finger and never licked them; he would give them a twist and they would stay tight. He would only smoke a few puffs, then throw it away and roll another.

"I do not know when Mr. Gordon came to this valley. I know he was here in 1896 or 1897. At different times he stayed at Billy York's hotel in Claryville, at DeMund's, and at Herron's, in Neversink, and for the last three years of his life he lived at Anson Knight's in Bradley [across the river from Neversink Village]. He always stayed in as good accommodations as there were in the locality, and so far as I can tell, he always had money enough to live on.

"While his mother was alive he used to stay winters at the Liberty House in Liberty, New York, with her, and in summer he would live in Neversink, Claryville [at the forks of the Neversink] or Bradley, close to the river. He would go from river to river in earlier years, staying a week or two at each place. In later years, probably because of his failing strength, he no longer went from one stream to another.

"He spoke to me quite a lot about his mother and what a care she had been to him. He would tell me about the English chalk streams, but I never understood that he had been in England. I do not know that he ever belonged to any club around here and do not know what club he referred to as the Flyfishers in his letters.

"He was a great friend of Bruce Leroy's, and sometimes he would stay with him. Bruce was always getting feathers and raising feathers for Mr. Gordon, and when Gordon would buy a good rooster he would give it to Leroy to keep for him. He would just pick out the feathers occasionally; Gordon never kept chickens.

"Mr. Gordon was a very fine fisherman. He did not cast a particularly long line in spite of the big rods he used, but he cast a particularly nice line, and he could cast the fly right where he wanted and put it down the right way. As I said before, he usually fished only to rising fish but sometimes, if he wanted exercise, he would fish when there were no rises. It should be remembered that in those days it was common to see a pool covered with jumping fish; it was nothing to take three or four out of one pool." (The terms "jumping" and "bugs" were very widely used by the older generation of trout fishermen; nowadays the words are more likely to be "rising" and "flies" or, perhaps, "naturals.")

"Mr. Gordon studied the insects and used to carry a little thin bottle of alcohol in his pocket; if he caught a bug he would take it home and try to copy it. He never used a marrow spoon"—this point was raised because of Gordon's friendship with Skues, who advocated the marrow spoon for extracting stomach contents from a dead fish—"but he would cut a trout open to see what it had been feeding on.

"There was a beautiful big pool at York's Ford that since has filled in; it was four or five feet deep in the middle and had a pothole fifteen feet deep at each end. Mr. Gordon went up there many a day to get the big trout that lived there. One day when the drakes were on, the big fish came up and Gordon said he took his fly 'like a blackberry.' When he 'squeezed the handle of the rod' to tighten on him, the fish was off; he was using drawn gut. Later, the big trout was caught at night in one of the nets that had originally been used to snare passenger pigeons. Bruce Leroy saw the fish taken" (and helped to catch it, according to Ed Hewitt). "It weighed over six pounds."

"If Gordon could get someone with a horse and buggy to drive him, he would be tickled to death to go up to the Big Bend or York's. He did not fish much downstream from Anson Knight's house, although there was a dandy night hole down there, only about three or four feet of water in it.

"One time I saw a couple of good trout in a hole about a mile below Neversink. It was a nice pool; the upper end was nice fast water, and there were some rocks for the fish to run under. I took Mr. Gordon down there, and he got one fish, a sixteen-inch fish, and I think I got the other one in Hewitt's Camp Pool, in the middle or latter part of June, at night on a No. 6 dun fly—dun hackle, dun-colored muskrat fur or seal's fur body, with hackle palmered down over it, and wood-duck wing. It was twenty-nine and half inches long and weighed eight pounds four ounces. I caught another one in the East Branch [of the Delaware] that was three inches shorter and two ounces heavier.

"Gordon did not fish at night, but he would go quite often for an hour or so after supper, in July and August. I remember once he caught a fish that weighed two pounds; he came up to the house and wanted to know if I would take it down to Smith's.

"Mr. Gordon used the Light Cahill and the Quill Gordon to imitate the drake. He tied them in three shades, and so do I. As the season advances, the hatch gets lighter in color. He would put on a big fly, Quill Gordon or Cahill, and fish for big fish just like any other trout.

"He used to fish the dry fly for bass just the same as he did for trout, down on the East Branch of the Delaware, between the towns of East Branch and Cadosia. He would take a boat and fish the big eddies [in the Delaware watershed a long, deep river pool is called an eddy] with big bushy dry flies. He would locate a rising fish and cast to it. When he located a big fish, he would study the stream, the bugs, etc., just as he did for trout. He went after one big bass that turned out to be a brown trout thirty inches long that he said would have weighed ten pounds, and that sounds about right." (Gordon released the fish, which is mentioned in his published works and letters, because the trout season was closed.)

"What Mr. Gordon did not like was to have his leader float. He certainly did hate a floating leader; he would not fish with one. He always soaked them well in water and was careful not to get any deer fat on them when he greased his line. He usually put a little kerosene on his fly.

"As a flytier, there is one outstanding fact about Theodore Gordon. He never taught anybody to tie; he never showed anybody anything, even me. When I went to his room, if he had a fly in the vise half-finished, he would take it out and lay it on the table. I used to show him flies that I made and sometimes he would say, 'That one ought to take a fish,' but he never would say anything about the way they were tied. He liked me, and he would make me flies, but he never would let me see him make a fly."

(The foregoing positive statement was directed against a once-famous Catskill tier, Rube Cross, who, Christian angrily said, told people he had learned to tie from Theodore Gordon.)

"Mr. Gordon tied the Quill Gordon, Light and Dark Cahill, and the pig's wool flies in light, medium, and dark colors. He used a wire over his quill sometimes for protection, not for color. He invented the Quill Gordon and the Gordon and a lot of other flies that he did not name at all. Many of the 'special' flies now in common use were invented by him." (A dig at Rube's famous Cross Special.)

"The story of Gordon's Bumblepuppy is that there was a fishing guide in Haverstraw who used a long cane pole to fish live bait in the weed pockets, for bass. Gordon tried to tie a fly that could be fished this way and after making three or four that were no good, he made one that caught fish. He made me one, but he did not make it big enough to suit me. I took it over to Loch Sheldrake and it caught fish, but no big ones. I made it bigger and a little different." (Hook 1/0 Model Perfect, mixed scarlet and white hackles, narrow brown turkey wing above thin white bucktail tied with butt of hair reversed, white chenille body, scarlet ibis tail.)

"I started to tie flies when Mr. Gordon got so he did not make me as many flies as I wanted. I could not get what I wanted in the store, so I started to tie my own. Nobody ever showed me anything about tying. I used my fingers—I still tie with my fingers and just put the fly in the vise a moment to finish it—and worked it out myself. The first time I ever saw anyone else tie a fly was when I was put in charge of Pflueger's flytying department, thirty-two or thirty-three women, in Akron.

"Some time around 1886, private people brought 2,000 brown trout from the Caledonia (New York) Hatchery and stocked the river. In a few years every hole in the river had three or four big fish in it, and it was nothing to see forty or fifty fish jumping; you could look them over and take your pick.

"Bruce Leroy and I stocked the river for twenty years. We would get all the farmers around to sign over to us their allotments of fry and fingerlings from the state, and we would meet the train with a horse and wagon and take the cans to the river and stock the fish.

"The Neversink was a fisherman's paradise around 1900. I cannot see much difference now in the river itself. But in 1900 it was nothing to see fifty trout jumping in a hole, and you could fish the river for a month without seeing a man unless it rained; then a few farmers would come down to fish with bait.

"The drake is the great fly in the Neversink; we do not have the Green Drake and the Coffin Fly [Gray Drake] of the Beaverkill. The male of our drake is a sort of smoky dun color, and the female is a big fly with spotted wings and a yellow body. The Quill Gordon imitates the male and the Light Cahill, the female. They come on about dark in great multitudes and fly upstream, and they look as if they had tails on each end—they have feelers sticking out in front."

(I am totally at a loss to identify this fly. I know the Never-sink no longer has the Green and Gray Drakes— (*E. guttulata*) —although the oldtimers said they occurred as far upstream as just above the Neversink iron bridge, when the banks were cultivated fields instead of second-growth, as they became. Christian's flies sound vaguely like the Hendrickson, which should be on much earlier than Decoration Day, however. The feelers sound like stonefly or caddis. And Ed Hewitt used to use and sell a wet fly with mottled brown and tan wings— female pheasant was Jack Atherton's guess—and a grayish-tannish body with, it seemed to me, a few shreds of green wool in it. Ed called it a stonefly, but I always thought it more resembled a caddis; it was tied with "down" wings, for one thing. It was a deadly fly on that river. After he died I checked with Farlow in London, who used to tie them for him by the gross; they had no record of the pattern. And none of those in the Anglers' Club who bought them by the handful had a surviving specimen. But I will say this: the Light Cahill, with almost whitish body as developed by W. A. Chandler and/or Rube Cross, is a really sterling fly on the Neversink, all summer long.)

"The drake comes on just about Decoration Day and is on all through June. I have seen them so thick you could not put your finger on the water without touching one. Usually they won't come out until dusk, but if it is a cloudy day, they may come on about noon and hatch three or four times during the afternoon. The fly is just about the size of a nice No. 11 artificial.

"I think you can never get a big fish to come to a dry fly except when the drakes are on. They won't pay any attention to little flies at all. I have caught three or four fish over twenty-two inches on a dry fly, and it was always when the drakes were on. That is about the limit in size that I have caught on a dry fly.

"Even in deep water, a big fish that is feeding will come up for a natural fly and not go down again very far; he will only go down maybe ten inches. You can almost always get a jump out of a fish that is feeding with a head and tail rise. And if you see a fish jumping today, you can go back tomorrow and see him jumping in the same place, at the same hour."

ROY STEENROD

When Roy Steenrod retired in 1952 after serving twenty-six years as a New York State fish and game protector, the affiliated sportsmen's clubs filled the biggest dining room in Sullivan County at a testimonial dinner which was the more impressive because a goodly number of those present had been pinched by him for hunting or fishing violations sometime during his career. He had won their respect and liking, as indeed he has that of all the regulars who fish in the western Catskills.

But it is the boys who best know and like this well-spoken, smiling, even-tempered man who does not now like to be reminded that in his youth he was a hot professional motorcycle test rider and a holy terror in a fist fight. As a master flytier (he created one of the best American brown trout flies, the Hendrickson) and lifelong fisherman, hunter, and woodsman, Roy has been counseling and instructing Boy Scouts almost from the beginning and holds the prized Silver Beaver of the organization for his services. And he has been teaching flytying and woodcraft in the state conservation seminars for boys at the DeBruce Hatchery ever since they were started.

A strictly home-grown product of Liberty, New York, Roy was born in 1882 of old American Revolutionary stock. He caught his first trout, right in Liberty, at the age of five and soon began taking all-day fishing trips, carrying a frying pan and a slice of bread so he could bring his catch home inside him. So it was natural that when, in 1904, he went to work in the United States Post Office, he should have become acquainted with Theodore Gordon through selling him foreign money orders with which to buy English flytying materials.

Roy feels that he was closer than any of Gordon's other friends, and one cannot interview him without sensing that this devoted friend is continually choosing what he will and will not reveal and is holding back personal and family matters which he undoubtedly feels it would be a breach of confidence to disclose.

More than all, Roy has one unique distinction. He is the only person to whom Gordon gave flytying instruction, aiding him from time to time with hints and tips which he was "on his honor not to tell anybody" and suggesting that Roy learn to tie without a vise so he could tie a needed pattern on the stream.

For it is a fact that Gordon jealously guarded his flytying knowledge, which, Steenrod thinks, he gained from books except for his exchanges with Skues.

Gordon's books, which his executor gave to Steenrod, testify to their owner's reticence and secretiveness. All but one of these are replacements of those destroyed by fire in 1913 while they were stored in Liberty, and as he died in 1915, there was not much opportunity for them to have become used. But even his old, well-thumbed copy of Francis Francis's *Book on Angling*, which he owned and used for many years, is devoid of any marginal comments, penciled notations, underscorings, or other reflections of their owner's personality. Apparently this does not reflect orderliness, which was not an outstanding trait of the owner, but secretiveness. "That was one thing about Gordon—he never put anything concerning his flytying methods or patterns any place where anyone could get hold of it," Steenrod explains.

The Gordon books owned by Steenrod are: Perry Frazer's *Amateur Rodmaking*, the gift of Mrs. C. F. Clark of Michigan, whose husband had been a copious Gordon correspondent (I believe it was Mr. Clark's large collection of Gordon letters that Mr. Clark's widow burned as rubbish, after having kept them for many years, a couple of months before John McDonald traced her down) ; two copies of George LaBranche's *Dry Fly and Fast Water,* one a gift to Gordon from Will T. Williams of Lebanon, Pennsylvania, another correspondent, and then to Steenrod "with the compliments of his friend Theodore Gordon" and the other inscribed "to Theodore Gordon, Esq., an angler and one whom I am glad to call my friend, this little book is inscribed with the best wishes and compliments of George M. L. LaBranche"; Emlyn Gill's *Practical Fly Fishing,* inscribed "to Theodore Gordon with the deepest appreciation of the unknown correspondent 'Whirling Dun' for the beautiful flies sent to him through Forest & Stream"; Ronalds's *Fly Fisher's Entomology* (rebound by Steenrod) , which apparently was bought secondhand in England, for it bears a penciled signature,

"Rev. H. Corles (?)" and a notation referring to the gray drake on an Austrian river; Halford's *Modern Development of the Dry Fly, Dry-Fly Entomology,* and *Dry-Fly Man's Handbook;* G. M. Kelson's *The Salmon Fly* "from R. B. Marston to Theodore Gordon with best wishes, Christmas, 1914"; Francis Francis's *A Book on Angling,* fifth edition, and Leonard West's *The Natural Trout Fly and Its Imitation.*

"Gordon came from the South," Steenrod recalls. "He had no particular Southern accent, but he had the manners of a Southern gentleman, talked often about Savannah, had quantities of mail forwarded to him from that city, and kept hackles in envelopes bearing his name and a Savannah address; apparently he had been in the banking business there. He did a lot of writing, and I often wondered whether he had been to college or had picked up his education himself. He did not get out often or mix much with people, but he was very fond of Bruce Leroy, and sometimes he would take trout to the A. W. Smiths, city people who had a big summer home near Herron's on the Neversink where Gordon boarded for a time.

"If Gordon liked you, it was all right, but if not, you had better keep out of his way; he was kind of a cranky old cuss. When I was working in the post office, I had Wednesday and Saturday afternoons off, and I seldom missed walking over to Bradley [about five miles] to spend the afternoon with him. When I did not, he would worry about me.

"Gordon's mother was a little bit of a woman, about as big as he was—five feet two inches. She used to come up to Liberty, and he would come over from the Neversink and visit with her for a week or two; she never went over there. His only relatives were apparently the Pecks in Haverstraw,

New York, and the Spencers in The Oranges, in New Jersey. One of the Pecks (probably Gordon, his favorite nephew, named for him) came to Liberty to fish with him a couple of times. At the end, when Gordon got so bad, he would not have a doctor, and I could not do anything with him. I got out of him the address of Robert Spencer in New Jersey and wrote to him to come up. Two brothers came up before Gordon died, and they came again afterward." Steenrod still has Spencer's letter of acknowledgment in which he agreed that he would not disclose that he had been sent for, and would not come to Bradley on the days when Steenrod would be there.

It will be noted that both Steenrod and Christian got in touch with Gordon's family shortly before he died. Both of their accounts are much too detailed and circumstantial to be figments of a failing memory; it is obvious to me that these contacts were made at approximately the same time, and that the cousins got in touch with each other and arranged to visit Gordon circumspectly so as not to alarm him.

"The only people present at Gordon's funeral besides myself were two men and two women, apparently relatives. Bruce Leroy was not told of the funeral and felt terrible afterward that he had not been present, and my recollection is that the same was true of Herman Christian," Steenrod continued.

"Gordon's mother was not present either, a fact upon which a letter from Gordon to me may shed light: 'My mother sleeps most of the time. The question is—has she strength enough to carry her through? I doubt if the doctor thinks so. She is surrounded by her nearest relatives, except myself, and the doctor thought my presence would excite and inspire her. I would have a bad time and probably be ill if I did go down there, and I could do nothing but be in the way.' "

One indication of Gordon's interest in Roy was his practice of asking him to write reviews of fishing books. "Then he would tell me: 'Young man, you had better not jump at conclusions.' When Emlyn Gill's book came out, he asked me to write a criticism of it, on which he made that same comment. He did not think much of the book," says Roy.

As a matter of fact, Roy inherited some of Gordon's correspondents. He had considerable correspondence in later years with R. B. Marston, the great editor of *The Fishing Gazette* in London, and with the widows of W. T. Williams and C. F. Clark, both of whom are mentioned in the published Gordon letters. One of Roy's regrets is that he did not preserve more of this correspondence, particularly with Gordon.

"Back around 1905 my correspondence with him was heavy, but it was only in the last few years of his life that I kept his letters. Even so, I have a lot that were not published. These were later given to Miss Kraft and are now in her possession."

These letters and Roy's close friendship with Gordon enable him to clear up several puzzling points in the published letters, including the identities of "C. M.," "the fat lady," and that mysterious stream the Ringip, which the closest study of Catskill region maps fails to show. "C. M." was Charles Messiter of Young, Messiter & Dodge, who had a general store in Liberty; he hunted with Gordon. "The fat lady" was Mrs. Anson Knight, with whom Gordon boarded in the last three years of his life. And the full text of the letter which mentions the Ringip makes it clear that Gordon was not talking about the Catskills, as the date might indicate, but about Rockland County, New York. "It is wonderful the fishing and shooting there is to be had within 40 miles of New York," Gordon wrote. "Three or four years ago a young relative of mine . . ." And in that anecdote he mentions the mysterious Ringip. Incidentally, the name is twice clearly written as beginning with the letter "P," but one cannot decipher whether it is "Pingip" or "Pinqip." The name is probably an old or local one, and the stream just possibly may be the one in Rockland County now known as Cedar Creek, still a good little trout stream. The confusion was heightened by the fact that there is a Cranberry Pond in Sullivan County and a Stony Clove over beyond the Esopus, as well as in the Haverstraw area; both were mentioned in the cryptic letter.

The one mystery which Roy cannot, or more likely will not, solve is the identity of the woman with whom Gordon was photographed fishing the Neversink, and the circumstances of its taking. He says that the published picture (in McDonald's book) and another, unpublished picture of Gordon and his friend reclining on the stream bank and apparently taken on the same excursion, turned up in one of Gordon's books after his death. Although there is no name on it, he thinks a professional photographer took it since it is a proof, brown in tone. But photographer's proofs are purposely not chemically fixed to make them permanent, and to have lasted so long it must have been "retoned" to a sepia tint, a photographic fad popular in Gordon's time. Roy is definite in saying that the picture was taken in the Neversink, several hundred feet above the old Neversink bridge, in the run alongside the road by the stone wall in front of Chandler's house. (All that is now under a hundred feet of water in Neversink Reservoir.) But that is all he will say; and all that Christian would say was that "Gordon was disappointed in love and the girl in the picture is the one; she was not a local girl—I don't know who she was." So probably we shall never know the identity of this intrepid sportswoman, and maybe it doesn't make much difference.

In discussing Gordon as an angler, Steenrod has the opinion that Gordon would not rank with the best present-day tiers in technique, but he says that Gordon's flies were unsurpassed in effectiveness because in his day he was one of the very few who understood the nature of the dry fly. He was meticulous about the quality of his hackles and about hooks, and he labored endlessly to achieve the exact shades to match the body colors of natural insects. "He continually asked me to get different colors of silk and wool for him from my sister's embroidery shop in Liberty," Roy recalls. He fell heir to Gordon's tying materials and still has many boxes of the Hall's eyed hooks that Gordon preferred, Gordon's tying vise, which Roy still uses, and a big bag of crewel wool in scores of shades.

"He was a good fisherman and, particularly, a careful stalker. He paid a lot of attention to the sun and things like that. He used a big rod but with a very light line; and although he did not cast far, he cast very delicately and put his fly on the water 'just so.' I think he learned to fish in Rockland County, but at that time he was mostly a bass and pickerel fisherman. He learned his trout fishing pretty much in the Catskills. The first I ever heard of him in the Catskills was around 1895.

"I think he fished downstream, wet, almost entirely until he fell under the influence of Skues and began fishing upstream. Then he fished half wet and half dry—*in* or just under the surface. Many of the flies which he originated and in which he specialized, such as the Quill Gordon, Catskill, and Gordon, represented classes of flies rather than particular species, but on some flies he was particular as to the color of the hackle, and on the body color it had to be a perfect imitation. His Quill Gordon was what we called silvery—almost invisible, 'water-colored.' "

Naturally, it is impossible to talk long with Roy about the old days without getting some comments about the fishing as it was then.

"In LaBranche's time there was mill after mill up the North Branch of the Callicoon from Hortonville to Callicoon Center —one dam after another, with big rainbows in the rough water under the falls.

"I fished often from Neversink to Hasbrouck, and there were eighteen- and twenty-inch fish there all the time," Steenrod continued. "About a mile below Neversink, opposite Frank Hall's farm, the river came right down against some big rocks, and there were a couple of ten-pound fish there all the time." (This was below the present reservoir dam; there is scarcely any water at all there now.)

"There used to be wonderful fishing in the Beaverkill. Everybody went up to Beaverkill Village and Lew Beach on the upper river, but I used to go down in the big water below the Junction [of the Beaverkill and Willowemoc]. You could go from Roscoe to the town of East Branch [about nineteen miles] and never see anyone in the river. You could resolve to take nothing under fourteen inches and still come home with all the fish you could carry."

This reporter had the distinction of spending a fishing weekend on the Beaverkill with Roy Steenrod in 1955, in the course of checking material for this article. We fished the

Schoolhouse, the Wagon Tracks, Baxter's, Cairns', and (above the Junction) Dow's Eddy in the middle of June without ever seeing a decent fish working, although the river was covered with rising chub and little eight-inch stocker trout— and spinning-rod fishermen. Some fifteen years after our interview the state ran Route 17, a famous traffic gutter, more or less down the bed of the Beaverkill from Roscoe to East Branch, the stretch of water Roy mentioned. Gordon did not survive to see what happened to his beloved rivers; Steenrod has. Which of them, after all, was the lucky one?

THE GRAVE OF THEODORE GORDON

"Time moves slowly in angling," John McDonald wrote in *The Complete Fly Fisherman.* But it moves rapidly in every other aspect of life, so that it was ten years after McDonald had published his opus and three after Miss Kraft had finished her investigations that the determination to clear up the one outstanding unknown fact of Gordon's history, the place of his burial, crystallized into action.

The situation which faced the researchers, Miss Kraft and the present writer, was that, first, there is no official, governmental record of Gordon's burial place and no record of any kind except in the files of the quiescent and obscure corporation that still operates the cemetery in which he lies. Second, there was no unanimity of recollection among the few aging people who might have known where Gordon was buried, including his relatives. And third, the recorded facts were meager and inconclusive.

The town clerk's records in Neversink Village showed the burial place as simply "New York." The fortunately preserved records of McGibbon and Curry, the Liberty undertakers who had handled Gordon's funeral, showed that his body had been shipped via the Ontario & Western Railroad, the day after the funeral, consigned to Gordon's nephew Robert Spencer of South Orange, New Jersey, and that it had been received by one Frederick Bommer, otherwise unidentified.

It is curious how a fixed, mistaken idea can arise and become accepted so firmly as to persist through the years, coloring and misleading all thought connected with a situation. In this case it was the conviction among a number who had had some connection with Gordon, including the undertaker and Gordon's friend Roy Steenrod, that the nephew Robert Spencer had retained an undertaker in The Oranges, Frederick Bommer, to inter Gordon's remains somewhere in or near South Orange.

The situation was further clouded by the "recollections" of friends. One aged woman was positive that the services had been held in the little church in Claryville, which is famous among Catskill anglers for having a wooden trout as a weathervane, and that Gordon was interred in its churchyard; she remembered looking in through the church windows to watch the services as a little girl. The established fact that at the time of Gordon's death an unusually late spring had left snow piled up to the windows of the house in which he had died and that the ground had been too solidly frozen for grave digging cast doubts on this recollection.

A number of others were sure Gordon was buried in Haverstraw, New York, where his relatives the Pecks lived and where he himself had stayed for several years. And an aged relative said that "he was buried in the family vault in some old New York cemetery" the name of which she could not recall.

Having checked the official records, the next step obviously was to check the cemeteries in and around South Orange, New

Jersey, and New York City and Haverstraw, New York. New York and Haverstraw were checked by Miss Kraft by telephone, but invaluable assistance in checking the South Orange cemeteries was volunteered by Mr. John Knapp, a long-established funeral director of that town. He even went to the length of having a cemetery employee make a personal check of the headstones in Robert Spencer's burial plot on the chance that Gordon might be in the plot without being in the records. All of these investigations were no less valuable for having drawn complete blanks.

The next obvious step was to identify Frederick Bommer and discover who had taken over his undertaking business and records. Here the investigators drew another blank. Telephone books and directories of The Oranges in or around 1915 were found not to be available. The licensing of undertakers in that area had not begun until 1927, so there was no help in that quarter. It was noteworthy that Mr. Knapp, who, as he said, "thought he knew everyone who had been in the business around here for the last forty years," could not recall a Frederick Bommer. The suspicion began to grow that Bommer might not have been an undertaker but merely a truckman who had transported Gordon's remains to some pier on the New Jersey waterfront from which it had gone by steamer to Alabama, where he had lived in his youth and where he had family connections.

"I believe his mother is the key to the situation," Miss Kraft said during a discussion. "They were very close; she protected and overprotected him all her life, as long as she was able. She visited him each summer in the Catskills almost up to the time he died. He never married. I wonder if they aren't buried together."

Her records showed that Fanny Jones Gordon had lived

in South Orange, and that she had died late in 1915. A look at the vital statistics in the South Orange Village Hall was obviously in order, and the present writer went over there for that purpose. Miss Mary Scully, a longtime employee in the Village Hall, a native of South Orange, and one of those people who know and remember everything and everybody, made short work of the search.

"Fanny Jones Gordon, aged 86 years 1 month, residing at 444 Hillside Place, South Orange, died of a cerebral hemorrhage and arteriosclerosis December 23, 1915, and was interred in the New York Marble Cemetery."

And what—and where—was that? Neither the telephone book nor the classified directory listed it. But Miss Scully called up a friend who was a funeral director, and he, after consulting some sort of directory or handbook, came up with the information that the cemetery was on Second Avenue and Third Street, Manhattan, and even furnished the telephone number of the superintendent. For good measure, he added the rather confusing information that several blocks away there was another cemetery, the New York *City* Marble Cemetery, not connected in any way with the other except that the superintendent was the same man!

This superintendent, Mr. Eugene Restucci, proved to be most obliging and helpful. His own records were complete, but he had been superintendent only since 1941, and his predecessor, he noted, had kept only fragmentary records or, usually, none. Mr. Restucci looked through what records were available and found plenty of Gordons in both cemeteries, but no Fanny Gordon or Theodore Gordon either. He called up the office of each corporation and quickly got negative reports.

But could not the headstones be checked? They could not, for like many oldtime New York cemeteries, both of these consisted entirely of underground vaults, each containing the ashes or remains of as many as forty people, and without identifying markers of any kind except that the name of the *owner* of the vault is inscribed above it on the cemetery walls. The only record of those interred in it would be in the books of the owning corporation.

Had not a New York City burial permit been issued? No. None had been necessary since a death certificate had been issued by the town clerk of Neversink Village.

By this time Mr. Restucci had become interested and volunteered to help.

"How much do you know about this whole thing?" he asked.

"Well," I said, "we know that the body was shipped from Liberty, New York, by train and received at the Weehawken terminal by a New Jersey undertaker named Frederick Bommer . . ."

"Frederick Bommer!" Mr. Restucci exclaimed. "He was no New Jersey undertaker! He had the job here before I did; he was a New York undertaker and the superintendent of the New York and the New York City Marble Cemeteries until he died!" And yet we hadn't found the grave.

"Sometimes people are careless," said Mr. Restucci. "I am going to try the offices again." Forthwith he called the secretary of the New York Marble Cemetery, who read to him over the telephone the following information from the corporate minute-book.

"At the first meeting of the directors in 1916 it was reported that among those interred in the New York Marble

Cemetery during 1915 were Fanny Jones Gordon and Theodore Gordon, both in the vault of George Gordon, No. 26."

There remained only to go to the scene. New York is an old city which grew from a small area, so that numerous cemeteries that were originally established in the outskirts have long since been engulfed. But even when they are filled, and all known relatives have disappeared, it is so difficult to "abolish" an old cemetery as to be virtually impossible. So long as there are funds for perpetual care, and space for further interments, the cemetery continues as a living entity even though its corporate soul may consist of nothing more than a set of books in a drawer of a lawyer's desk.

The New York Marble Cemetery occupies the interior—what otherwise would be the back yards—of a square block of tenement houses, small stores, humble dwellings (several of them over a century old) and a municipal lodging house for vagrants. The block is between Second and Third Avenues and Second and Third Streets, a distinctly shabby neighborhood in 1957 but vastly changed from the ghetto of fifty years ago that centered around it and made infamous such streets as Cannon, Rivington, Delancey, and Hester.

The only outward sign of the cemetery is a locked iron gate in an arch between two buildings which leads into a passage closed at the farther end by another locked gate. Through the gates a stretch of high retaining wall and a fragment of grassy turf are visible. The little half-acre cemetery itself is flat and unencumbered, well grassed, neat and seemly; the retaining wall and the absence of back yards deprive urchins of both incentive and opportunity to invade the premises.

A week before the forty-second anniversary of Gordon's death on May 1, 1915, Roy Steenrod and I went to the sloping shore of Neversink Reservoir, behind and above the site of the old Anson Knight house, and there gathered an armful of laurel. We gathered another beside the Brooklyn Fly-fishers Club water on the Beaverkill, where Gordon had loved to fish and where he had been a permanent permittee.

I had a wreath made from this doubly symbolic greenery, and on May 1, 1957, Miss Kraft and I hung it below the marker which stands at the head of the vault, on the wall. Later in the month when Roy Steenrod was in New York as the guest of The Anglers' Club at its Spring Dinner, The Theodore Gordon Society along with Miss Kraft, John McDonald, and Roy, visited Gordon's grave and the occasion was recorded by photography.

WHO WAS GORDON?

Virginia Kraft's research has produced what few personal facts are available about Theodore Gordon, and I am indebted to her for permitting me to use some of them herewith; but the stated conclusions from those facts are mine alone, and differ in some respects from hers.

Briefly, Gordon's mother was Fanny Jones, of an upstate New York family but born in Pittsburgh; after being orphaned at an early age, she was raised by an aunt and uncle in Mobile, Alabama, in better than average comfort and social status. There she met and in 1850 married the darkly handsome Theodore Gordon, of an old New York City family, who was in the South for his health. Apparently they returned at least briefly to Pittsburgh, for our Theodore Gordon was born there in 1854; but four months later, in 1855, his father died in Mobile at the age of thirty, the stated cause of death being malaria.

With money getting low and local feeling against Northerners rising, the widow returned in 1860 to Pittsburgh to live with kinfolk, the Spencers. Here the six-year-old Theodore spent what were undoubtedly the happiest years of his life, for the Spencers had a summer farm at Carlisle, Pennsylvania, in an area that was then a paradise for fishermen and hunters and even today is not too far from meriting that description. Theodore, with his cousins Charlie and Bob, roamed the woods and fields from dawn to dark; in those years he gained the knowledge of shooting and fishing and the great love of nature and passion for the outdoors that remained with him as long as he lived.

Winters in Pittsburgh were another matter; Theodore was subject to heavy colds, pneumonia, and kindred ailments so that his mother became increasingly distraught and protective. As time went on she curtailed his school attendance and, increasingly, his summer outdoors activities until he became, according to those who knew him then, moody, sullen, frustrated, and withdrawn.

Soon after the Civil War, his mother took Gordon back to the South and by 1880 had decided to settle permanently in Savannah, Georgia. It is a pity we do not have more light on that crucial ten-year period of a young man's development; it might solve the mystery of the source of Gordon's undeniably good education, for one thing. In Savannah he appears to have worked sporadically as a bookkeeper and later as either a securities dealer or the branch manager of some securities firm. Meanwhile, his mother was tutoring him in the niceties of the Southern culture in which she had been raised, and laboring frantically, in the face of approaching poverty, to maintain and augment his entrée to polite society and to introduce him to an endless succession of socially advantaged and financially secure Southern belles.

By 1893, Gordon's health and financial resources, and his customers' investments, had all pretty well failed. So he and his mother came north and for a while lived with the Spencers, who by then were in South Orange, New Jersey. Apparently Gordon worked from time to time in New York brokerage offices—his letters intimate as much—but whenever he could raise the funds he would disappear, a couple of months at a time, to fish the Pennsylvania and Catskill streams. When his money ran out he would go to his father's relatives, the Pecks, in Haverstraw, New York, and the senior Peck would give him a job of some sort to tide him over.

About 1900 the rest of his health failed, and he went to live permanently with the Pecks, eventually having flytying and sleeping quarters in a detached building where he could be alone. It will be noted that even then Gordon was tying flies for the market, at least to some extent. He learned the art from Thad Norris's book.

He and one or another of the Pecks had been going to the Catskills on fishing trips from—according to local recollections there—about 1895 on. Now their visits became longer, and in 1905 Gordon decided to stay up there permanently, probably for financial no less than health considerations. His mother attempted to protect him as long as she lived; as long as she was able to travel, she would go up to Liberty each summer and stay there for a few weeks while Gordon would come in and stay with her. Eventually she became too feeble, and too far removed from reality, to continue this practice and ultimately she died without ever having been told that her son had predeceased her.

Upon several points all of the people interviewed by Miss Kraft or by me seem united. One was that Gordon continually, and often bitterly, complained about his mother "and what a care (burden, trouble)" she was to him. It is most unlikely that he ever contributed substantially to her support. She, on the other hand, wore herself out and devoted her whole life to trying, on the one hand, to get him to take care of a grave chronic illness and on the other, to find a wife who would support him. It seems to me that, even allowing for his natural boyhood frustrations, he was an unappreciative and ungrateful son. And his rather whining alibi to Steenrod for not going down to be with his mother in her last days—that his presence would only "excite and inspire" (he meant stimulate) her, that the doctors held out no hope for her, that he could do nothing for her and would only be in the way, and that he would become ill himself, indicate a substantial degree of selfishness, and an absence of affection for his own mother. There are many extenuating circumstances, but I know a host of sons who, in like circumstances, would let nothing keep them from their mother's side.

"They were both frail, impractical people, incapable of coping with the world," one relative told Miss Kraft, and I can't think of a description that apparently better fits the facts. Under all the circumstances, I think it is a great tribute to Fanny that she was able to accomplish so much, as long as she did. The last thing she did for him was to reveal to posterity, through the record of her own death, the place where her son is buried.

Another point of general agreement among the relatives is that Gordon was fond of his small nieces and nephews and they of him.

"We kids liked him." "He was always considerate of youngsters." "He'd talk to us and tell us how to hunt and fish." "I used to sneak up to his room over the garage and watch him tie flies; people say he'd never let anyone see how he tied his flies, but that's not true. He used to let me watch and sometimes he'd show me how to wind the silk." "He had a great deal of patience with children. His mother stayed several summers with him at Liberty, New York, and I sometimes went up to visit them. I remember the delicious trout he would catch and cook for our supper at the hotel." "On one occasion he brought a guinea pig in his pocket for the children." Those are some of the comments of persons who knew him as children.

On the other hand, there is universal agreement among those who knew him in the Catskills that he was brusque, gruff, sharp-tempered, and "cranky" except with the apparently few people whom he liked. But no hint of all this appears in any of his letters or writings that have survived.

Finally, there is general agreement among the relatives that Gordon was addicted to liquor; but agreement just as general among his Catskill friends that he was abstemious in this respect. The explanation is simple: The relatives who so well remembered his drinking all grew up in a social stratum and a time when "taking a drink" was a thing to be done rather furtively and considered not quite respectable. Any drinking at all was a lot, to them.

And if Gordon showed the effect of it (which he usually did by opening up and conversing interestingly on all sorts of topics, for he was well read) , consider that he weighed about ninety-five pounds, and calculate how much liquor it would require to knock such a man off his feet. One and all, they mention Gordon as gruff, brusque, silent "until he had had a drink." It was his medicine for overcoming the repression and frustration which normally kept him silent.

It is significant that I cannot find anyone in the Catskills (where nothing—*nothing*—is secret from the natives) who thinks of Gordon as a drinking man; both Christian and Steenrod are specific on this point, and I don't think they are covering up for him. When Gordon was in fishing country he just wasn't repressed or frustrated. He lived only for fishing, shooting, flytying, and the appreciation of nature; when he had those he was happy.

And perhaps the best reason of all for his temperance was that he never had the price. Steenrod says that Gordon never had more than four or five dollars at a time; "if he got a few dollars ahead he'd immediately set up a fishing trip somewhere," he told me.

The Theodore Gordon Society were disappointed when they were not allowed to provide and affix to the wall above the Gordon vault a little bronze commemorative plate. But after all, only the very least of Theodore Gordon lies in Vault No. 26. The most, and all of the best, of him has remained alive in the memories of anglers since the day he died. And his best memorial is composed of the innumerable numbers of his flies that innumerable fly fishermen cast onto innumerable waters, every day of the open season, year after year after year.

(The mysterious Pingip discussed on pages 147 and 148 is undoubtedly one of the unnamed streams rising on Mount Pyngyp, near Haverstraw, New York, we learned at press time from Mr. Robert H. Boyle, an authority whose fascinating book, *The Hudson River,* has recently appeared.)

THE INDOMITABLE

ALL WAS QUIET ALONG THE RIVER AS I CAST MY FLY UP INTO the pool, but before it floated back, battle had been joined in the next valley. The forces of heaven were attacking over there, for I could hear the war drums of the thunder. Reeling up hastily, for these mountain storms come fast, I waded ashore and took shelter under a hemlock.

It was a brief engagement. The forces advanced rapidly, and in a few minutes rain topped the high crest and charged with flashing bayonets down upon the valley. It stamped the river flat and passed over the thick woods with the sound of a marching multitude. With it came the lightning running a brilliant scale like bugles sounding the charge, and thunder for the accompanying drums. Clouds scudded by like massed battle flags.

The storm passed over, the thunder sounding the long roll beyond the crests until it died in the distance, but the rain continued to march steadily past like the train of an army.

Behind me the river frothed under it; it slashed the dirt in muddy streams from the gravel of the narrow path before me and dripped steadily through the branches onto the thirsty moss. A wet, earthy odor arose.

Suddenly the close unstirring air was pierced by a military summons whistled with martial vigor; far up the path sounded the notes which a leaping memory identified as "First Call for Guard Mount." The whistler was evidently no recruit; he knew army routine, for it was succeeded by "Assembly" and then by the plunging cadences of "Adjutant's Call." A sharp command followed, then a series of stirring bugle marches. He was mounting the guard. "You're in the Army Now," "Payday," "There She Goes"—an old soldier this, one who had walked many a post, for these were all favorites of the Old Army.

Now the sound of footsteps came to me under the hemlocks. Striding feet they were, firmly set down in the marching cadence. Now they were breasting the rise from the little meadow, but the marcher had breath to command "Sound off!" in a carrying voice and then break into the whistled strains of "Zamboanga."

Now he was in sight, a big man, square and well set up. His lined, ruddy face was wet with rain. Rain plastered his flannel shirt to his shoulders, his breast was black with it, and his back was streaming. Above his boots his trousers were sopping, and my ear detected the squelching of wet feet in cadence with the thud of his heels. Behind his hip a creel rode so lightly as to suggest that it was empty, and in his right hand he bore the joints of a fishing rod upon the butt of which an automatic reel was still mounted. With this rod he thrust rhythmically before him in the arm-swing of a marching soldier.

The man was as wet as if he had been in the river, but he did not know it. His face was composed, even pleasant, and his eyes held a faraway look. With wings on his ankles and drums in his heart he was striding across some sun-baked parade ground. He never saw me.

"Route order—*march!*" he commanded and then loudly, unmelodiously but with unquenchable spirit, broke into song. The years fell away, and I saw again a brown line of packed and helmeted figures streaming along a white road, for the song he sang was "Mademoiselle from Armentières." The charging rain beat against that song, broke, and turned back. The trees took it in their arms and meshed it in their leaves. The river bubbled in time with it.

He was past, now, the grinding of the gravel under his heels growing fainter. The bawdy words and rollicking tune sounded farther off. Now he came to the turn of the path.

"An officer came across the Rhine, parley-voo,
An officer came across the Rhine, parley-voo . . ."

The well-remembered words trailed into indistinguishable sound, and the sound into silence. I heard again the marching of the rain and the dripping of the branches.

I took the pipe from my mouth and saluted. It was a sentimental indulgence, but I had just seen a brave man. I have said that he was swinging his right arm, but I failed to add that he was not swinging the left. That sleeve was empty.

* * *

The foregoing fantasy was written many years ago as a tribute to the indomitable crippled veterans of my world war who were making new successes of their lives despite seemingly insuperable obstacles. I would like to add now the account of an incident which I witnessed in Halloran General Hospital after the Second World War, as my tribute to the crippled veterans of the succeeding generation.

Here came two kids jockeying their wheelchairs down the corridor with the expertness, spirit, and almost the speed of dirt-track racers. They were bound for the telephone booth beside which I stood, and it quickly developed that, with one nickel and one telephone number between them, they purposed to call up some girl and kid her five cents' worth. Along came a nurse, young and, easy to see, a favorite of the troops.

"What," she demanded amiably, "are you guys up to?"

The younger of the two—they were both heartbreakingly young—broadened a grin already wide and flipped a hand in an airy gesture.

"Just roving around," he said jauntily, "looking for adventure."

Adventure! A game leg and a wheelchair apiece, one telephone number and one nickel between them. Adventure? Yes, for they had, besides, high indomitable hearts in which and only in which the true spirit of adventure dwells.

I did not salute because it would have embarrassed them.

MURDER

"IF FISHING INTERFERES WITH YOUR BUSINESS, GIVE UP YOUR business," any angler will tell you, citing instances of men who lost health and even life through failure to take a little recreation, and reminding you that "the trout do not rise in Green Wood Cemetery," so you had better do your fishing while you are still able. But you will search far to find a fisherman to admit that a taste for fishing, like a taste for liquor, must be governed lest it come to possess its possessor; that an excess of fishing can cause as many tragedies of lost purpose, earning power, and position as an excess of liquor. This is the story of a man who finally decided between his business and his fishing, and of how his decision was brought about by the murder of a trout.

Fishing was not a pastime with my friend John but an obsession—a common condition, for typically your successful fisherman is not really enjoying a recreation, but rather taking refuge from the realities of life in an absorbing fantasy in which he grimly if subconsciously reenacts in miniature the unceasing struggle of primitive man for existence. Indeed, it is that which makes him successful, for it gives him that last measure of fierce concentration, that final moment of unyielding patience that in angling so often makes the difference between fish and no fish.

John was that kind of fisherman, more so than any other I ever knew. Waking or sleeping, his mind ran constantly on the trout and its taking, and back in the depression years I often wondered whether he could keep on indefinitely doing business with the surface of his mind and fishing with the rest of his mental processes—wondered, and feared that he could not. So when he called me one spring day and said, "I'm tired of sitting here and watching a corporation die; let's go fishing," I knew that he was not discouraged with his business so much as he was impatient with its restraint. But I went with him, for maybe I'm a bit obsessed myself.

That day together on the river was like a thousand other pages from the book of any angler's memories. There was the clasp and pull of cold, hurrying water on our legs, the hours of rhythmic casting, and the steady somnambulistic shuffling that characterizes steel workers aloft and fly fishermen in fast water. Occasionally our heads were bent together over a fly box; at intervals our pipes wreathed smoke; and from time to time a brief remark broke the silence. We were fishing "pool and pool" together, each as he finished walking around the other to a new spot above him.

Late afternoon found me in the second pool below the dam, throwing a long line up the still water. There was a fish rising to some insect so small that I could not detect it, so I was using a tiny gray fly on a long leader with a 5X point. John came by and went up to the Dam Pool, and I lost interest in my refractory fish and walked up to watch, for there was always a chance of a good fish there. I stopped at a safe distance and sat down on a rock with my leader trailing to keep it wet, while John systematically covered the tail of the pool until he was satisfied that there were no fish there to dart ahead and give the alarm, and then stepped into it.

As he did so his body became tense, his posture that of a man who stalks his enemy. With aching slowness and infinite craft he began to inch up the pool, and as he went his knees bent more and more until he was crouching. Finally, with his rod low to the water and one hand supporting himself on the bottom of the stream, he crept to a casting position and knelt in midcurrent with water lapping under his elbows, his left sleeve dripping unheeded as he allowed the current to straighten his line behind him. I saw that he was using the same leader as mine but with a large No. 12 fly.

"John, using 5X?" I breathed. Without turning his head he nodded almost imperceptibly.

"Better break off and reknot," I counseled softly, but he ignored the suggestion. I spoke from experience. Drawn 5X silkworm gut is almost as fine as a human hair, and we both knew that it chafes easily where it is tied to a fly as heavy as No. 12, so that it is necessary to make the fastening in a different spot at frequent intervals in order to avoid breaking it. I kept silence and watched John. With his rod almost parallel to the water he picked up his fly from behind him with a light twitch and then false-cast to dry it. He was a good caster; it neither touched the surface nor rose far above it as he whipped it back and forth.

Now he began lengthening his line until finally, at the end of each forward cast, his fly hovered for an instant above a miniature eddy between the main current and a hand's breath of still water that clung to the bank. And then I noticed what he had seen when he entered the pool—the sudden slight dimple denoting the feeding of a big fish on the surface.

The line came back with a subtle change from the wide-sweeping false cast, straightened with decision, and swept forward in a tight roll. It straightened again in front of the caster, whispered through the guides, and then checked suddenly. The fly swept round as a little elbow formed in the leader, and settled on the rim of the eddy with a loop of slack upstream of it. It started to circle, then disappeared in a sudden dimple, and I could hear a faint sucking sound.

It seemed as if John would never strike although his pause must have been but momentary. Then his long line tightened —he had out fifty feet—as he drew it back with his left hand and gently raised the rod tip with his right. There was a slight pause and then the line began to run out slowly.

Rigid as a statue, with the water piling a little wave against the brown waders at his waist, he continued to kneel there while the yellow line slid almost unchecked through his left hand. His lips moved.

"A big one," he murmured. "The leader will never hold him if he gets started. I should have changed it."

The tip of the upright rod remained slightly bent as the fish moved into the circling currents created by the spillway at the right side of the dam. John took line gently and the rod maintained its bend. Now the fish was under the spillway and must have dived down with the descending stream, for

I saw a couple of feet of line slide suddenly through John's hand. The circling water got its impetus here, and this was naturally the fastest part of the eddy.

The fish came rapidly toward us riding with the quickened water, and John retrieved line. Would the fish follow the current around again, or would it leave it and run down past us? The resilient tip straightened as the pressure was ended. The big trout passed along the downstream edge of the eddy and swung over to the bank to follow it round again, repeated its performance at the spillway, and again refused to leave the eddy. It was troubled and perplexed by the strange hampering of its progress, but it was not alarmed, for it was not aware of our presence or even of the fact that it was hooked, and the restraint on it had not been enough to arouse its full resistance.

Every experienced angler will understand that last statement. The pull of a game fish, up to the full limit of its strength, seems to be in proportion to the resistance which it encounters. As I watched the leader slowly cutting the water, I recalled that often I had hooked a trout and immediately given slack, whereupon invariably it had moved quietly and aimlessly about, soon coming to rest as if it had no realization that it was hooked.

I realized now that John intended to get the "fight" out of his fish at a rate slow enough not to endanger his leader. His task was to keep from arousing the fish to a resistance greater than the presumably weakened 5X gut would withstand. It seemed as if it were hopeless, for the big trout continued to circle the eddy, swimming deep and strongly against the rod's light tension, which relaxed only when the fish passed the gateway of the stream below. Around and around it went, and

then at last it left the eddy. Yet it did not dart into the out-
flowing current but headed into deep water close to the far
bank. I held my breath, for over there was a tangle of roots
and I could imagine what a labyrinth they must make under
the surface. Ah, it was moving toward the roots! Now what
would John do—hold the fish hard and break it off; check it
and arouse its fury; or perhaps splash a stone in front of it
to turn it back?

He did none of these but instead slackened off until his
line sagged in a catenary curve. The fish kept on, and I could
see the leader draw on the surface as it swam into the mass
of roots. Now John dropped his rod flat to the water and
delicately drew on the line until the tip barely flexed, moving
it almost imperceptibly several times to feel whether his
leader had fouled on a root. Then he lapsed into immobility.

I glanced at my wristwatch, slowly bent my head until I
could light my cold pipe without raising my hand, and
then relaxed on my rock. The smoke drifted lazily upstream,
the separate puffs merging into a thin haze that dissipated itself imperceptibly. A bird moved on the bank. But the only
really living thing was the stream, which rippled a bit as it
divided around John's body and continually moved a loop
of his yellow line in the disturbed current below him.

When the trout finally swam quietly back out of the roots,
my watch showed that it had been in there almost an hour.
John slackened line and released a breath which he seemed
to have been holding all that while, and the fish reentered the
eddy to resume its interminable circling. The sun which
had been in my face dropped behind a tree, and I noted
how the shadows had lengthened. Then the big fish showed
itself for the first time, its huge dorsal fin appearing as it rose

toward the surface and the lobe of its great tail as it turned down again; it seemed to be two feet long.

Again its tail swirled under the surface, puddling the water as it swam slowly and deliberately, and then I thought we would lose the fish, for as it came around to the downstream side of the eddy it wallowed an instant and then headed toward us. Instantly John relaxed the rod until the line hung limp, and from the side of his mouth he hissed, "Steady!"

Down the stream, passing John so close he could have hit it with his tip, drifted a long dark bulk, oaring along deliberately with its powerful tail in the smooth current. I could see the gray fly in the corner of its mouth and the leader hanging in a curve under its belly, then the yellow line floating behind. In a moment he felt of the fish again, determined that it was no longer moving, and resumed his light pressure causing it to swim around aimlessly in the still water below us. The sun was half below the horizon now and the shadows slanting down over the river covered us. In the cool, diffused light the lines on John's face from nostril to mouth were deeply cut, and the crafty folds at the outer corners of his lids hooded his eyes. His rod hand shook with a fine tremor.

The fish broke, wallowing, but John instantly dropped his rod flat to the water and slipped a little line. The fish wallowed again, then swam more slowly in a large circle. It was moving just under the surface now, its mouth open and its back breaking water every few feet, and it seemed to be half turned on its side. Still John did not move except for the small gestures of taking or giving line, raising or lowering his tip.

It was in the ruddy afterglow that the fish finally came to the top, beating its tail in a subdued rhythm. Bent double, I crept ashore and then ran through the brush to the edge of the still water downstream of the fish, which now was broad on its side. Stretching myself prone on the bank, I extended my net at arm's length and held it flat on the bottom in a foot of water.

John began to slip out line slowly, the now beaten trout moving feebly as the slow current carried it down. Now it was opposite me and I nodded a signal to John. He moved his tip toward the bank and cautiously checked the line. The current swung the trout toward me and it passed over my net.

I raised the rim quietly and slowly, and the next instant the trout was doubled up in my deep-bellied net and I was holding the top of it shut with both hands while the fish, galvanized into a furious flurry, splashed water in my face as I strove to get my feet under me. John picked his way slowly down the still water, reeling up as he came, stumbling and slipping on the stones like an utterly weary man. I killed the trout with my pliers and laid it on the grass as he came up beside me; and he stood watching it with bent head and sagging shoulders for a long time.

"To die like that!" he said as if thinking aloud. "Murdered —nagged to death; he never knew he was fighting for his life until he was in the net. He had strength and courage enough to beat the pair of us, but we robbed him a little at a time until we got him where we wanted him. And then knocked him on the head. I wish you had let him go."

The twilight fishing, our favorite time, was upon us, but he started for the car and I did not demur. We began to take off our wet shoes and waders.

"That's just what this depression is doing to me!" John burst out suddenly as he struggled with a shoelace. "Niggling me to death! And I'm up here fishing, taking two days off in the middle of the week, instead of doing something about it. Come on; hurry up. I'm going to catch the midnight to Pittsburgh; I know where I can get a contract."

And sure enough, he did.

NIGHT FISHING

HEAT AND FEAR OPPRESSED THE LAND, FOR IT WAS ONE OF those stifling, humid August nights when the whole countryside is awake and every living thing is abroad on the business of life and death. The darkness was so thick and close that one tried instinctively to push it aside, and the air was heavy with the menace of predators and the terror of their prey. The river was soundless save for a faint spattering at my feet, a mere whisper which I could not identify until I turned on my little flashlight and discovered in the very margin of the stream, where it feathered off to nothing on a sandy beach, a dark line of what appeared to be stranded twigs and chaff. It was a horde of the tiniest of minnows, which had taken refuge in the ultimate edge of the water and still leaped frantically over each other in their efforts to be farthest from the prowling fish they knew would soon be seeking them.

I waded across the broad river to where a little cold feeder entered it and began to cast a big black wet fly on a heavy

leader, for this is the season when the hellgrammites rise
from the river bottom and swim ashore to pupate under stones
before hatching into huge nocturnal dobson flies. It was too
early yet for big fish to be feeding, but there might be a
stray around, and anyway, I wanted to be fishing. So for a
couple of hours I inched along silently on felt-shod feet working my fly in the cooler water along the bank, where a fish
might be harboring. At midnight it was still hot and breathless. Perspiration dripped off my face, and inside my high
waders I was soaked with it. I was weary of swinging the big
ten-foot fly rod, too, so I went ashore and sat down for a
while before I made my way up to the head of the long
pool.

The sky had somehow brightened now, and the darkness,
so thick and close before, appeared thin and luminous. It
seemed as if I could see farther than I really could, but at
least I could make out the stranded log on the far bank shining as white as bone. I replaced my wet fly with a deer-hair
bug to imitate some blundering moth and began to work out
line along my side of the river. It is difficult to get out in
darkness just the length needed to reach one's target but
not impossible if one is familiar with the water and his rod,
so when I picked up the cast and pushed it straight across at
the log, I was confident that my bug would drop right in front
of it.

I brought my hand down hard and the bug smacked the
water. A white flower of foam blossomed in front of the log,
and blossomed again when I swept the tip back in a hard
strike. I was into a fish! It headed down the current, and I
held the rod high overhead and reeled desperately to take up
the slack. I seemed to be choking, and it took me a moment

to discover that it was because I was holding my breath.

Alas, the fish was strong but not strong enough; fighting but not fighting hard. Suspicion at once changed to conviction, and conviction became certainty when I brought the fish into the circle of strange pale light cast by the little flashlight which by now I held between my teeth. It was a chub—an alderman, the grandfather of all the chub in the river, a chub as round as a rolling pin, one with pretensions to rise above his class and act like a trout, but still . . . a chub.

I unhooked and returned him—gently, because I was grateful to him for providing a little action; stowed away my flashlight and felt for my pipe. Only then did I realize that my heart was pounding slowly and heavily, like a burned-out main bearing.

That is night fishing, the essence of angling, the emperor of sports. It is a gorgeous gambling game in which one stakes the certainty of long hours of faceless fumbling, nerve-racking starts, frights, falls, and fishless baskets against the off-chance of hooking into—not landing necessarily or even probably, but hooking into—a fish as long and heavy as a railroad tie and as unmanageable as a runaway submarine. It combines the wary stalking and immobile patience of an Indian hunter with sudden, violent action, the mystery and thrill of the unknown, a stimulating sense of isolation and self-reliance, and an unparalleled opportunity to be close to nature since most creatures are really nocturnal in habit.

Above all, it provides the stimulation of sudden fright at the startling things which continually occur in the dark, and in fact I incline to believe that that is the greatest lure of the sport. In all of the night-fishing experiences that I recall, the outstanding thing was always that I was scared half to death.

Of these experiences, two are notable.

I used to prowl around in the deep still water where a small brook entered an ice pond, fishing for big rainbows that worked up into the stream after dark. The banks were swampy and in the stream the mud was knee-deep, but there was firm bottom under it and I could work along an inch at a time, wading almost to the top of my armpit-high waders onto the boot feet of which were strapped hobnailed leather sandals.

Saplings grew shallow-rooted on the marshy banks and were continually falling into the stream, so when, this night, I encountered the tip of one that had sunk into the mud, I thought nothing of it and backed away. The trouble was that the point of the sapling had run under the strap of my sandal and, having a knob on it, was stuck and could not be withdrawn. I soon found that I could not break the thing off because it was too flexible, nor drag the whole tree loose because it was too firmly anchored by its roots. So the situation was that I was tethered by the foot twenty feet from shore in mud so thick that I could scarcely move my feet and water so deep I had to move cautiously to avoid filling my waders. And it was darker than the inside of a coal mine.

It was a simple and rather ridiculous plight, but I could see very little about it that was humorous, particularly when I reflected that I was beyond shouting distance of a house or a road. In fact, after I had thoroughly tested the possibilities of getting loose I emitted a little cold perspiration in spite of the warmness of the night.

The only thing I could think of to do—which was to discard my rod, dive down and use my hands to free myself—was neither promising nor inviting. It would leave me flat in the stream with my waders full of water and my feet stuck deep in the mud, probably confused as to the direction in which the bank lay—and I can't swim. If I were unable to regain my feet and my balance in the darkness, and that seemed very likely indeed, I would be in a very perplexing situation. I had also to consider the possibility that I might not be able to free my foot; in that case I would have even less freedom of movement of my legs to assist me in regaining and keeping a vertical position.

I haven't the remotest idea how long I stayed there—it seemed hours—but all the while I was cogitating I was also twisting my foot and flexing the twig. Eventually it either broke off or pulled out, and although I was even keener for night fishing then than I am now and still had plenty of time left, I headed upstream to the hauling-out place at my best speed. And as soon as I got ashore I unstrapped the sandals and hurled them into the bushes. I have never since worn anything when wading at night, under or in which a stick might catch.

My other memorable experience was the result of several varieties of folly. It was early May on the Beaverkill and I had not found fish, so, misled by the warm sun and balmy air, I thought there might be night fishing in my favorite pool, the Wagon Tracks. Normally Cairns' Ford, at the head of the pool, is almost out of water except for a little channel close to the road side of the stream, but now I found it knee-deep all the way across, pants-pocket deep in the channel and of course running like a milltail. It was a tough crossing in daylight; I did not stop to think what it would be like at night.

I found that what was normally the shallow side of the

pool had been scoured by floods, and in the high water I had to wade close to the bank. It was not a good sort of night water in that condition, but I was still bemused, so I put on a big stonefly nymph and started working down, casting straight across and letting the fly swing round, then fishing it back close to the bank, an inch at a time. I worked along on numbing legs for hours, staring blankly into darkness relieved only when a car passed along the road on the other side. The water was quiet, dead in fact; and then I thought I felt a light touch on the nymph, right below me, just as it would be finishing its swing. Action at last! Surely something had lipped the nymph; that was just the right point in its swing to expect it. Could I make the fish come again?

Reeling up the slack I had already worked in so that my next cast would come to exactly the same length, I chucked the nymph across the current again, and as it began to swing I unconsciously leaned forward with my arms extended in an attitude of hair-trigger alertness. The line straightened and I knew the big nymph swinging behind it was approaching the spot. Now . . .

Something, a mink perhaps, leaped off the bank and struck the water right under my outstretched arms; as it hit, a good-sized fish leaped out and made its escape.

I stood fixed; I couldn't have moved to save my life. The sweet, sickening taste which is the real flavor of fear filled my mouth and my heart hammered in my throat. I began to strangle and knew I was holding my breath, but I could not command my lungs to function.

When I had recovered the power of movement I decided that I was through, took down my rod and got my little flashlight out to go back across the ford. Now the ford ran at a diagonal and my target was a clump of bushes on the other bank. I couldn't see the bushes with my little light, but I could see the stream bottom—the shallow ford and the deeper water on either side of it. So I went along all right for perhaps a quarter of the way, and then my flashlight played out.

I had only a couple of hundred feet to go, more or less, but that is a long distance when the water is too high, the night too dark and the way too uncertain. I worked ahead feeling for the shallower water but soon got into the position familiar to every night fisherman in which one seems to be surrounded by deeper water. All right; I would stand still until a car came along to shine its headlights on my brushy marker. But this was wartime, with gasoline rationing in force, and people were not driving much at night. I think only the fact that it was Saturday night, traditional "night out" for countrymen as well as city folk, saved me.

I stood there a while beside that short, ugly rapid roaring down into deep water, remembering that I couldn't swim even without high waders and heavy hobnailed shoes to handicap me. Then a car flashed by and I found my marker and stepped out boldly until once more I seemed to be hemmed in by deep water. As I recall, I had to wait for four cars in order to reach the edge of the deeper channel, ten feet from the bank.

I stepped down into it cautiously with one foot, found a rolling stone, dislodged it, and got solid footing; I brought the other foot forward, worked it in and out of some sharp-angled pockets, and planted it beside the first. The water was halfway above my knees now, tearing at my legs, growling and foaming. The steep pounding rapid was white in the darkness and what I could see looked as bad as it sounded.

I shuffled a foot forward, then brought the other one up beside it; the water was an inch deeper. I felt and withdrew with first one foot and then the other, then inched half a step downstream to get around something high and slippery. I completed another shuffling step. At last I was just two steps from safety, one into deeper water and the next up onto the bank. I put the rod joints in my mouth to have both hands free and resolved to throw myself forward and grab for bushes if I felt myself going. I took a deep breath and stepped out, and as so often happens, anticipation was worse than reality. My foot held, and in the next instant I was hauling myself out.

I sat down on the running board of my car, filled my pipe, and looked at my watch. It was 1:00 A.M. daylight saving time. My feet were numb, my legs ached, and my mouth was dry, and when I took off my waders I discovered that my knees were trembling slightly but steadily and uncontrollably. Fatigue? Not on your life. I was scared stiff.

NOCTURNE

It is curious that the most vivid memories of a fisherman are those of sight rather than sound. Let him consider
the incidents he remembers best and he will realize that they
came to him through the eye rather than the ear. Its very
uniqueness, then, is an additional reason for cherishing a
memory that came to me entirely through the ear. It is an
incident of which I heard all and saw nothing.

I was camped on the Willowemoc beside one of those pools
that redeem the stretches of broad shallows characteristic of
the Catskill rivers in summer. The midnight stars furnished
just enough light to reveal the flying bat and the laboring
moth. Baked stones and lifeless brush still yielded their
heat, but an edge of coolness was creeping into the breathless
air. In the shallows the river trickled silently.

I was at last almost asleep when I heard a faint recurring
sound up the river. As I listened it came closer and soon I
could identify the swish of a fishing rod and the crunch

and rattle of stones shifting under the feet of someone wading along the stream. Clatter, clatter, clatter. Swish-swish. A pause. Then the same succession of sounds again.

It was a night fisherman. The level beds of these flood-swept Catskill rivers, loosely paved with small stones and gravel, are smooth enough for wading in the dark. A few fishermen make a practice of doing so in the hot weather, fishing a bucktail or a large wet fly for the big trout which at that season feed only during the cool hours.

I looked out of the opening of my tent, but the brush was too thick for me to see the unknown fisherman without rising. So I lay in my blanket listening idly for the sound of a hooked fish and half wishing that I too had gone fishing.

The Unknown was a workmanlike angler. The grinding of the stones and the recurrent swish of his rod told me that he was systematically covering the water, taking the regulation three steps between casts. There was no interruption to his steady progress except the brief pause to fish out each cast. Now he was opposite me, skirting the pool. Clatter, clatter, clatter. Swish-swish. A pause while he slowly retrieved the lure. Clatter, clatter, scramble—SPLASH!

A tremendous floundering, a rasping of hobnails, a rending of the waters as he emerged, and the sound of dripping garments came to my ears. And then the night was shattered by a spate of profanity from such springs of bitter passion as are tapped only by such a catastrophe. All the disappointment of a fishless night, all the strain of hours of wading, all the primitive, instinctive fear of the dark joined with the shock of a sudden fall and an involuntary immersion to dash the Unknown's self-restraint.

I listened in admiring silence. I have heard an apoplectic

sergeant of six enlistments drilling rookies. I have heard a regular army stable detail unloading a car of bad actors from the remount station. Once I heard a high officer ask the driver what was in a stalled truck that was blocking the ammunition going up and the wounded coming back, and when the driver replied, "Officers' baggage, sir," the high officer stood up in his sidecar and loosed a blast that fairly unloaded the offending bedrolls into the ditch.

Best of all, I once heard a gray-headed chief of section on maneuvers extricating an overturned caisson from a nest of rocks under the quiet, sinister admonitions of Charles Pelot Summerall, then a major, afterward chief of staff, and always a prime man-eater. That was swearing! "For the love of the bald-headed, paralytic . . ." began the sergeant in a trembling voice and then ascended to such heights of oratorical frenzy that we stood spellbound. When he sprang into the saddle with a final ". . . and six men and a corporal with sidearms for pallbearers," we knew we had heard the voice of a master.

But compared to the Unknown, these perorations were as the lisping numbers of little children. Louder and louder, higher and higher rose his eloquence, shocking the darkness and affrighting the landscape, until at last he stood upon the mountain peak and hurled a livid, blinding blast at the embarrassed moon. It was the climax. Gradually he slid down from the heights until at last he subsided into a morass of common hells and damns. Silence crept timidly back.

Then the Unknown resumed his progress down the river. Clatter, clatter, clatter. Swish-swish. A pause. Clatter, clatter . . .

With an envious sigh, I turned on my pillow and embraced sleep.

THE PERFECT ANGLER

I NEVER SAW HIM; IF ANYONE ELSE EVER DID, IT HAS NOT BEEN reported. I don't believe he exists. But if he did, what would his attributes be?

If we accept the little girl's statement that piano playing is easy—"you just press down on those black and white things" —and apply it to trout fishing, all it involves is:

1) finding a fish
2) deceiving it into taking an imitation of its food
3) hooking, playing, and landing it.

The first requirement is the most important; my guess is that finding a fish is anywhere from 50 percent to 80 percent of catching it. Overwhelmingly, the reason why so many experienced and well-equipped fishermen catch so few trout is that most of the time they aren't fishing over fish.

Bill Kelly, a research aquatic biologist and a skillful, experienced angler, says I should specify a *feeding* fish. If he means a big fish, I agree. "To catch a five-pounder, you must be there when he's feeding," Ed Hewitt once told me. And experts like Herman Christian agree that a good hatch of big flies must be on for about half an hour before the larger fish, over sixteen inches, will come on the feed.

Also, if Bill means the rich Pennsylvania limestone streams or the lush British chalk streams, I agree. But most of our eastern trout waters are hungry streams in which the smaller fish, up to maybe twelve inches, tend to harbor between hatches close enough to a feed lane to seize anything edible that may come riding down the current.

Anyway, finding a fish is the problem; the rest is patience.

Fish-finding is done by sight; by knowing the kinds of places in which fish harbor or feed; or by the simple hammer-and-chisel process of fishing one stretch so often that eventually one learns where the fish are, without knowing or caring why. The first method is the rarest, the second the most difficult, and the third the easiest but most limited.

Really fine fishing eyesight is a gift of the gods, the rarest and most enviable attribute a fisherman can possess, and I have never known a truly great angler who did not have it. Edward R. Hewitt had the eyes of an eagle, right up to his death; so did George M. L. LaBranche. And Ray Bergman's ability to see fish was so instinctive that he never could understand why everyone couldn't do it.

The hawk-eyed angler sees not only the fish themselves but the faint, fleeting signs of their presence—the tiny dimple in the slow water next the bank which indicates a big fish sucking down little flies; the tiny black object momentarily protruded above the surface, which is the neb of a good, quietly feeding fish; the slight ruffling of the shallows by a school of minnows fleeing from the bogeyman.

George LaBranche claimed in *The Dry Fly and Fast Water* that the knack of seeing fish under water can be learned by practice, but I incline to believe that either one is born with sharp eyes or one is not. On the other hand, there is a mysterious mental aspect of eyesight; sometimes it seems to be a quality separate from mere keenness of sight—visual acuity. Resolving power, the ability to see what we look at, seems to be a mental as well as a physical attribute. How else can we account for the almost incredible ability of the great British angler-writer G. E. M. Skues to discern whether trout were nymphing immediately *under,* or taking spent flies *in,* the surface film, when we know that he was virtually blind in one eye and had to aid the other with a monocle? Of course, knowledge plays a part. "The little brown wink under water," as Skues called it, means a feeding fish to the initiate but nothing at all to the tyro, just as that Pullman-plush patch in yonder bush, eighteen inches above the ground, means a deer in summer coat to the woodsman but is never noticed by the city yokel looking sixteen hands high for a hatrack spread of antlers.

The second method of finding fish, by learning to be "a judge of water," is to my way of thinking the highest attainment in this aspect of angling. Anyone who is willing to do the work can make himself a fair judge of water; like piano playing, a little of it is a simple thing to acquire. But mastery of the art is granted to but few, and a lifetime is not too long to achieve perfection.

It is remarkable what a good judge of water can do. Gene Russell, who learned the angler's trade on hard-plugged public streams around New York City, doesn't even set up a rod when he gets out of his car to fish a new piece of water.

He just saunters along the bank for half a mile or so, smoking a pipe and looking; then he saunters back and either drives away or gets out his rod and goes to one, two, or maybe three places which he has mentally marked down during his stroll.

What did he see? Maybe it was a tiny patch of watercress on the opposite bank, or perhaps moisture on a rocky face above the stream; either would indicate a seepage of cold spring water below which a fish is apt to be lying in hot weather. Maybe it was a big stone in the current—not any stone but one so faced and undercut that it creates an eddy of quiet water in front of it in which a trout can rest at ease while the stream brings him his vittles. Maybe it was a smallish trout exposing himself where no trout ought to be, on a clean sand bottom in brilliant sunlight. If there is a good lie nearby, the chances are that a bigger fish has driven the little fellow out of it; he wants to go back but daren't.

Maybe Gene saw a long stretch of shallow, brawling water, the natural feeding grounds of the trout, without any cover for a sizable fish anywhere along it except one hollow about as big as a bathtub. Maybe such a fish is using it for an advanced base.

More likely, Gene didn't really *see* all this, for an experienced, capable angler's stream sense becomes a part of his subconscious. Probably all he *saw* were a few places that seemed to say: try me.

The third method of fish-finding, that of learning a piece of water by experience, is, of course, a limited one, and yet it is remarkable how many miles of water an industrious and wide-ranging fisherman can learn by heart. I once heard the late John Alden Knight and a man named Crane, of Deposit, New York, testing each other's knowledge of some ten miles of excellent fly-rod bass water on the West Branch of the Delaware between Deposit and Hancock. They checked each other stone by stone on every pool and disagreed but once—as to whether there were four or five stones at the head of the Cat Pool. They finally agreed that there were five, but that there never was a bass behind the first one.

Still, the angler who depends on experience to know the stream is like the applicant for admission to the bar who had read nothing but the laws of the state. "Young man," thundered the judge, "some day the legislature may repeal everything you know." The stream is continually repealing much of what the local angler has learned; after every big storm, with its attendant filling of old holes and digging of new ones, he has to learn the water anew.

Thus far we have been able to follow a firm path. But it ends on the shores of an illimitable sea of controversy when we come to the second requirement of angling: to deceive the fish into taking an imitation of its food. Fortunately, it is not necessary for us to wet much more than the soles of our shoes in this sea.

First let us consider a few fundamentals. The trout is a very primitive creature with only two primary instincts. One is the spawning urge; it comes during the closed season so we need not consider it. The other is self-preservation. It cannot be emphasized too strongly that the trout spends all its time at the business of staying alive.

Unfortunately for the trout, its internal economy is such that it is never very far ahead of starvation; and the larder of the stream is not in the safest but in the most dangerous, i.e., exposed, places. The whole "food chain"—plankton, insects, minnows—lives in the fast, shallow places where there is lots of sunlight and quickly changing water. So when a fish gets hungry enough, it has to risk itself out where the food is. Aside from food, it has only two other requirements—oxygen (as you know, it is dissolved in the water) and cover—protection from its enemies and shelter from such elements as floods and ice. Obviously, the only instinct of the trout to which the fisherman can appeal is its appetite; the only lure which will interest it is an imitation of its food.

Trout eat about every living thing that they can catch and swallow, but in the main they feed on smaller fish and the various life forms of water insects. There is something in the composition of water insects that makes them preferred by the trout to any other form of food. But a big fish, which eats more, in proportion to its weight, than a man, just doesn't have the time or the energy to collect its nourishment one insect at a time, so it is forced to feed considerably on minnows, frogs, crawfish, and other sizable mouthfuls. But it is the glory of the brown trout that he never entirely ceases to feed on insects, no matter how big he grows, so that the fly-fisherman always has a chance—not a good one, but a chance —of setting his hook in the biggest fish in the stream. For the purpose of this article we shall assume that "food" means stream insects in their several life forms.

So to catch a trout the angler must deceive it into taking an imitation of some form of stream insect. There is a lot of dynamite in those two simple words "deceive" and "imitation," for they are the keys to the most uncompromising and violent disagreements in the whole world of sport.

Let us consider imitation first. The trout, being essentially a very simple creature, does not go through elevated mental processes in feeding but depends upon its reflexes; it has more automatic controls built into it than a guided missile. (They work a lot better, too.) It reacts to the approach in, or on, the current of an insect larva or winged fly according to the triggering of these automatic controls, varying with the circumstances. So imitation can only mean: whatever deceives the reflexes, the automatic controls, of the fish, *according to circumstances.*

That is an important qualification. An invitation to dinner doesn't look anything like a dinner, but, under different circumstances, each may bring a hungry man a-running. The angler may use a replica of the natural insect, complete even to its eyes, like Halford, or depend mostly on where he casts his fly and how it floats, like LaBranche, to deceive the fish. But if he does deceive the fish, that's all that counts; who will say he is wrong? For the purpose of our hypothetical perfect angler, it is sufficient to say, as regards imitation, that he knows how to imitate the natural food of the trout so well that the fish is deceived under every circumstance.

This involves a great knowledge of both aquatic biology and stream entomology and a great skill in expressing this knowledge in the concrete form of artificial flies. Our perfect angler must have the technical knowledge of such authorities as the late Dr. James G. Needham and his son Dr. Paul R. Needham (*Life of Inland Waters* and numerous other works, jointly or severally), and the late Dr. Ann Haven Morgan (*Field Book of Ponds and Streams,* and others). And like Theodore Gordon, who was probably the first man to fish the dry fly in America, our perfect angler must have a large practical knowledge of stream insects and the ability to construct imitations of them.

Imitation of the fish's food, the stream insect, is only a part of deceiving it; the rest is presentation, which involves stalking —getting into casting position without alarming the fish—and casting, including also fishing out the cast.

Stalking is another of the fundamentals upon which one may judge the quality of an angler. The real expert is always willing to credit the fish with the inordinate wariness which it always manifests, and he is willing to take the trouble to stalk as he should, even if it is no more than taking pains to scare the little fish in the tail of the pool downstream, out of the way, rather than upstream where they will alarm the bigger ones.

The great Skues was well into his eighties, an enfeebled old man, when he wrote to a friend that he "found it increasingly difficult to adopt an attitude of becoming reverence to the fish." British chalk streams usually can't be waded, and, typically, their banks are bare except for a few bushes to which the angler creeps and behind which he kneels to cast. Skues was finding it "increasingly difficult" to do so; but he was kneeling, nevertheless.

Over on what used to be the "railroad" side of Cairns's Pool on the lower Beaverkill, there was a magnificently deep, boulder-lined run that was just right for big fish. Every day during the season, literally scores of fishermen flogged that run, carelessly and ineffectually, from the shallow, "road" side. It couldn't be fished properly from that side and they knew it; they just wouldn't bother to do it right.

But for an expert like Harry Darbee, it was not too much trouble to cross the stream above the pool, walk along the railroad track, slither down a dauntingly steep and loose embankment, and then work from one to another of the huge rough rocks that protected the railroad fill from floods. With the stream on his left, his casting arm had to contend with an abominable mess of high bushes, low-strung telegraph wires, poles, and the embankment itself, and most fishermen said it wasn't worth it. But I saw Harry perched like a chamois on one steep-faced boulder after another, holding his rod across his body and making niggling backhanded casts to every good spot within reach.

Seldom indeed will one see the average fisherman crawling to reach the right spot, or kneeling in the stream to reduce his visibility; but Ray Bergman used to wear out the knees of his waders before any other portion, and Otto v. Kienbusch not only fished but progressed upstream on his knees along a quarter mile of the flat, gravel-bottomed, fish-infested upper Nissequogue on Long Island. Otto was one of the few who could get into the big browns in that stretch.

Every dry-fly man knows that there are ways of casting a curve or loop in his line so as to allow his fly a natural float when he is fishing across varied currents. But Ray Bergman was speaking important truth when he told me: "Curves are too hard to throw and succeed too seldom for you to bother with them. For every fish there is one place from which you can cast to him with a straight line and still get a free float. Figure out where it is and go there even if it means walking back a hundred yards to cross the stream and come up the other side." My lady wife, who can fish like an otter, heeded well this advice. Although she learned her fishing from a whole galaxy of expert casters and anglers, she has never even tried to cast a curve. She wades around until she finds the right place and then makes the short straight cast which, too often for the comfort of my ego, takes a fish.

Having stalked the fish, the angler must now cast, and

here all hell breaks loose, for there is more misconception, disagreement, and prevarication about casting than any other part of the sport. For one thing, practically no fisherman knows how far he really can cast, a fact which once nearly broke up one of the older Beaverkill clubs.

The clubhouse is right on the bank, and at noon the members come in for lunch and discuss the morning's fishing at the table. One low miscreant got tired of listening to these tales. Secretly he drove two stakes in the bank, a measured sixty feet apart. Next lunchtime, the first member to voice a standard fish-story remark—"I made a medium cast, about sixty feet—" was challenged by the miscreant. Bets were made, and the whole party repaired to the riverside, where an appalling thing was quickly discovered. The storyteller couldn't cast sixty feet, and, what is worse, none of the others could either. Since it is obviously impossible to tell a fish story without mentioning a sixty-foot cast, the members lunched in gloomy silence until at last they rebelled, chucked the beggar out, and went back to making sixty-foot casts at the luncheon table.

As a matter of fact, long casting is not of much use in trout fishing, at least in the East. Few, indeed, are the times when an angler really has to make a cast longer than forty-five feet, and fewer still the times when such a cast raises *and hooks* a fish. But if distance is not necessary to the angler's cast, control—the ability to cast accurately and delicately—is. Accuracy is a prime necessity when obstacles make it difficult to reach the fish. When deep water, overhanging trees, or the lack of room for a backcast forbid the use of that best of all fish-getters, the short straight cast, the angler must resort to high art flavored with black magic—the skillful manipulation of rod and line which so defies analysis and classification that it is called, simply, tip work.

George LaBranche likely may have been the greatest of them all at this, his forte. His preference was for smallish water, and the limitations imposed by so restricted an environment required him to perform blackest magic with the tip. It is a revelation to watch the tip work of an artist like Guy Jenkins, whose almost imperceptible manipulations seem to endow the fly with independent ability to guide its own flight among bushes and brambles and still achieve a perfect float.

Delicacy is the other half of control. The average fisherman cherishes the delusion that his casts place the fly on the water as delicately as an alighting insect. But if he casts on still water so that he can walk down for a close look at his fly, he probably will be distressed, as I have been, to see that it is awash *in,* rather than riding high *on* the surface film. The reason, I think, is that most fishermen still believe in that ancient chestnut which one fishing writer has copied from another ever since the dry fly became popular. It is that the caster should check his line while his fly is three or four feet above the water and "allow the fly to flutter down onto the water like an alighting insect."

This is so much bilge, tosh, sheep-dip, and hogwash. Even without a line or leader attached to it, an artificial fly cannot be dropped onto the water "as delicately as a natural insect alighting" or anywere near it, any more than you could do the same thing with a seaplane. Every winged creature uses its wings, and uses them a lot, in effecting a landing; a flying duck can make a beautiful three-pointer, but a shot duck can hit the water so hard he bounces. The instant and universal popularity which fan-wing flies and long-hackled spiders achieved in the 1920s was due to the fact that their larger sail area permits them to parachute down slower and more gently than an ordinary fly when they are checked high in the air and allowed to drop.

George LaBranche had the most delicate presentation of any angler whom I have ever observed. In his books, George speaks repeatedly of checking the fly in the air to get a delicate delivery, but what he did was really more than that. He made each cast, short or long, with a deliberate powerful stroke; checked the line hard so that the fly whipped down until it was only an inch above the water, with its headway killed; and then seemed to lower it gently, through that remaining inch, onto the water. On short casts, he could put his fly on the surface before line or leader touched the water.

To sum up presentation: In this, as in imitation, our synthetic perfect angler must meet one test—the exacting standards of the trout. He must be able to stalk and cast so well that he always deceives the fish.

The final angling requirement—hooking, playing, and landing the fish—is universally slighted both in practice and in the literature, in spite of the axiom that a sale does the store no good until it is rung up on the cash register.

The average fisherman's record on big fish is brief and dismal. He loses practically all of them that rise to his fly, and on the average it takes him less than five seconds apiece to do it. He hits them too hard and holds them too tight; that's the whole story.

Striking and playing a fish correctly is a matter of iron self-discipline and rigid control of one's reflexes. One of the greatest examples of it that I know of is Tappen Fairchild's conquest of "Grandpa," a four-and-a-quarter-pound brown trout that each year in late summer was driven by the warming of the upper Neversink to take refuge in a little ten-foot feeder stream that is always 46° F.

There was just one pool, about fifty feet in diameter, in this little spring brook, and in it this veritable whale lived, nervous and wary because of its restricted, dangerous quarters.

Tappen studied that fish for most of two seasons. He was a very tall man, and he had arthritis, but whenever he found time, he *crawled* to the edge of the pool and *knelt* behind a bush in order to study, hour after hour, the feeding and harboring habits of this fish. He found that its lie was under a submerged, fallen tree on the other side, and that when feeding, it worked round the pool, vacuum-cleaning occasional nymphs off the sandy bottom.

The trout was patrolling like that when Tappen finally went after it. Of course, laying a line anywhere near the fish, no matter how gently, would have sent it flying in panic. So Tappen cast a small nymph on 3X gut and let it sink to the bottom while the fish was at the other end of the pool. Imagine the mounting tension as he watched this enormous fish turn and start feeding back toward him. The faintest movement of rod, line, or lure would have sent it bolting off, but Tappen knelt like a bronze statue while the fish approached the nymph, inspected it, picked it up, started away with it, and by its own movement pulled it into the corner of its mouth and hooked itself!

The fish lashed the pool into foam when it felt the iron and darted irresistibly in among the sunken tree branches. Tappen backed off into the meadow so as to be out of sight, pointed his rod at the fish, and with his left hand gave a couple of very delicate, gentle pulls on the line. The fish quietly swam out the same way it had gone in.

To top it off, Tappen had lent someone his net. So he had to play his fish until it was broad on its side and completely exhausted, and then crowd it against his leg while he gilled it with his middle finger and thumb, thus completing a perfect demonstration of angling technique.

The tactics of playing a fish, like those of warfare, depend almost entirely on the "terrain," and it is difficult to establish doctrine on them, but there are a few principles on which knowledgeable anglers seem to be fairly well agreed.

Holding a fish hard when it is first hooked lets it break off.

"Let him go; tear line off the reel and throw it at him; don't put any pressure on him at all. He won't go far—maybe fifty yards," Ed Hewitt used to say. "Don't try to check that first run."

The time-honored adjurations to "keep the tip up" and "don't give any slack line" should not be observed strictly. They may be wrong or they may be right; it depends on the circumstances.

In order to breathe with any facility, a fish must face the current; even when migrating downstream it lets the current carry it tail first so it can breathe readily. So when a fish starts to take line downstream, it won't go far at any one time. Try to lead it into slacker water at the side of the stream. When a fish gets below the angler, it can hang in the current, breathing comfortably and doing no work to maintain its position. In this situation it is simply recuperating; unless the angler can get below it and put it to work, his chances of losing it are good.

A fish going straight away from the angler with the leader

over its shoulder is like a horse in harness, in the best position for pulling. If it is held hard, it may easily break off. But a fish swims as a snake crawls through the grass, by moving its head from side to side and using its broad body surfaces against the current. A light sidewise pull will so hamper this serpentine movement that it will quickly abandon its effort and turn aside. Where there is room, it is possible to keep an active fish turning almost continuously in a figure-eight pattern and thus prevent it from dashing downstream or into a hole.

It takes long to tire a fish by swimming; the angler seeks to drown it by maintaining steady upward pressure so as to tire its jaw muscles and force its mouth open. A fish has to close its mouth to squeeze water through its gills; when it can no longer do so, it quickly drowns.

The harder a fish is held, the harder it fights; if pressure is released entirely it will stop fighting and swim around aimlessly or rest on the bottom. A fish that is held too hard tends to sound, or go to the bottom, and sulk, jerking its head like a bulldog. This is hard on tackle and the hold of the hook; lightening the pressure will encourage the fish to come up and make an active, hence tiring, fight.

After the first five seconds of hooking and fighting his fish, the angler's greatest chance of losing it is through trying to net it before it is completely exhausted and broad on its side. Usually he unfurls his net immediately after hooking the fish. As soon as he can drag the still vigorous trout within range, he extends his rod hand far behind him, assumes a position like a fencer lunging, and extends the net at arm's length like a tennis player trying to stop a low shot. In this position the angler goes to work with his net like a man chopping down a tree, and unless his fish is well hooked and his leader sturdy, he's going to lose his prize.

Charlie Wetzel is the best netter I ever saw. He uses one of those big "snowshoe" nets, and he doesn't even get it out until the fish is on its side and completely tuckered. Standing erect, facing upstream with his elbows at his sides and his rod held just back of vertical, he sinks the net deep and draws the fish over it. Slowly, gently, he raises the rim of the net, tilting it from side to side to free the meshes from the fish's fins. Then he quietly, deliberately lifts the fish out of water, and it lies in the net as if hypnotized until Charlie grasps the upper meshes to hold it shut. It doesn't go into its final flurry until too late.

To sum up, we must require our hypothetical perfect angler always to hook his fish perfectly, in the corner of the mouth; to maintain utter, absolute control over his own reflexes, and to play and net the fish without committing an error.

Now we have constructed the perfect angler, but he's dead. To bring him to life we must infuse him with the spirit of a great angler. That is *not* the relaxed, gentle, lackadaisical spirit which delights in birds, flowers, wild animals, clouds, and the sweet clash of running waters. I have known great anglers who were thus benign, but it was not the spirit of their formative years, the thing that made them great, but a luxury which they could afford after fishing had ceased to challenge them. Ed Hewitt pinpointed it when he said: "First a man tries to catch the most fish, then the largest fish, and finally the most difficult fish." After that, the birds and flowers.

The spirit which makes the great angler is compounded of

terrifically intense concentration and a ferocious, predatory urge to conquer and capture. What less would drive Dick Jarmel, a well-known Beaverkill fisherman, to risk a bad battering and possible drowning by working his way for fifty yards along the retaining wall of the Acid Factory Pool, holding his rod crosswise in his mouth and clinging with fingertips and toes to rough projections of stones, simply to get to *the* spot from which the run can be fished effectively during high water?

Or impel Tom Collins (Ed Hewitt once called him the best fisherman ever) to climb down the face of a cliff, swing across a cleft on a rope affixed to a branch, and shinny down a convenient tree, all to get to a secret spot on a secret stream, down in a gorge? Tom had the heft of a grizzly as well as the strength and endurance of one, and he risked a broken neck and stove-in ribs time after time, as a matter of course. I laugh when I hear a doctor approving fishing as light recreation for a heart patient without finding out what sort of fishing it will be. He thinks of his man as soaking a worm while he dozes on the bank; he would be shocked to see, as I so often have, the hard-case angler coming in at eventide limp and sweat-soaked from prowling and galloping along the stream all day.

The furious urge of the great fisherman expresses itself in an intense competitive spirit. Some anglers conceal it very well, but it is there nevertheless, so strong that it can even bias their devotion to the truth. I still grin privately at what happened long ago when two really great anglers, who must remain nameless here, met by chance on a certain pool. They got into a discussion of wet fly versus dry fly and set up an informal competition, each fishing the pool in turn. I've heard the story from each of them, and you'd never guess that they were both talking about the same event. The only thing they agreed on was the name of the pool.

Ed Hewitt and George LaBranche were always tilting at each other. When both of them were aged men, Ed and I went up to George's office to surprise him one day. The two really dear old friends fell upon each other, and then George asked Ed what was new. Nothing, said Ed, except that he had another grandchild.

"How many grandchildren have you?" asked George. Ed fell for it.

"Eight."

"That's one thing I can beat you at," crowed George. "I have twelve."

Ed's eyes darted about as he sought furiously to redeem his defeat.

"How many great-grandchildren have you?" he demanded. This time George was under the guns.

"Five."

"Hah!" cried Ed triumphantly. "I have twenty-one!"

George's secretary looked shocked and beckoned me into the hall.

"Mr. LaBranche doesn't have twelve grandchildren!" she whispered.

"That's all right," I reassured her. "Ed doesn't have twenty-one great-grandchildren, either. They're just trying to beat each other."

Some twenty-five years ago I met on the stream a then well-known fishing writer, the late Albert C. Barrell, who, it developed, had fished a lot with LaBranche on the Konkapot in Massachusetts.

"George is a duelist," he explained. "The fish is his antagonist, his adversary. He'll return it to the water after he has conquered it, but he attacks it as furiously as if he were fighting for his life."

Here then, out of the zeal and the skills of many experts, we have synthesized the perfect angler. In the flesh this perfect dry-fly fisherman does not exist, and it is doubtless a good thing that he does not, for surely he would be intolerable to all us imperfect anglers.

THE LOTUS EATERS

No record remains of the early history of the club which a group of wealthy Brooklyn brewers and trout fishermen incorporated as The Fly Fishers Club of Brooklyn. But the late Chancellor Levison, who was a member, told Dick Hunt that the group fished Brodhead's Creek from the Henryville House in the seventies, and when the brook-trout fishing played out there in the nineties, moved to the Beaverkill and made their headquarters at Ben Hardenburgh's farm.

Legend says that Ben built a log cabin on his farm for a wealthy man who wanted a love nest; that after Ben had discovered what was going on and had run him off, the Brooklyn fishermen took it over for a dormitory; and when they had a mass disagreement with Ben some years later, they formed their own club and bought the cabin for their clubhouse. At the same time, the club took its pick of the trout water for a price little more than the traditional red apple.

As now constituted, the club has several acres of rolling

ground on the eminence of which is the same log cabin, with a separate mess hall behind it; two and a half miles, both banks, of the sweetest dry-fly water on the entire length of the Little River, more than half of it in fee and the rest on long-term lease; privileges of entry and water supply in connection with the late Ben Hardenburgh's farm; and a sound, well-built dam at the foot of the Home Pool which goes out with the floodwater each year.

The charter provides for twenty-five members, but unwritten law limits membership to twenty, the present number; after a lapse of many years, there actually is now one member from Brooklyn. The shares of stock, one to a member, are valued at one hundred dollars each and the dues are twenty-five dollars a year, besides an assessment whenever the dam goes out. But to stem any rush for the bargain represented by this combination of superb fishing and low cost, it should be noted that a flaming sword bars the entrance to this angler's Eden. It is the membership, the most unique thing about this unique institution.

For these are the lotus eaters. They live in a little world apart, a world which they found perfect upon entering and which, consequently, they strive to keep unchanged. Does there come one with wealth and social position? They do not comprehend the terms. Angling genius, and the prestige of authorship? They glance up incuriously and return to their concerns. Sportsmanship, pleasing personality, fellowship of spirit? They regard him with unfocussed eyes and murmur that they already have these qualities in the club. Here is one institution by which it is no reproach to be blackballed, for the present members are all agreed that if they themselves were now outsiders coming up for membership, they would be blackballed without exception. This is not a manifestation of caprice, misanthropy, or sadism. It is merely the outward expression of the spirit of the club, that everything is perfect the way it is—let us keep it that way.

This passion for the past carries the members to inordinate lengths, some of which may be described. For instance, the great one-room cabin bears no wall decorations except a thousand nails at which one may pitch his kit and hang it up, a series of penciled outlines of big fish, and a grocery store calendar for the year 1910. Even to stretch a hand toward this ancient, fly-specked relic elicits outraged cries and warnings from all present. The rough board floor is covered with a mud-caked rug of nondescript color; when Malcolm Runyon and the present writer essayed to remove and beat the tattered fabric, Scotty Conover, doyen of the club, leaped upon it in a heroic attitude and exclaimed, "That rug was put down in 1912, the year I joined the club. It has never been off the floor since, and it is not going to be taken up now!" The fireplace below the foot-thick flagstone mantelshelf contains a layer of ashes at least a foot thick. We removed a few inches of this deposit before we were discovered and restrained, and although we finally escaped expulsion, we never wholly lived down the opprobrium that descended upon us.

A new member who naïvely offered to have the cabin wired for electricity at his own expense shocked the members into literal speechlessness, and his sacrilege was blamed for a crack that appeared in the fireplace. The club's shame is the handsome new (twenty-year-old) mess hall, which had to be built simply because the old one had burned down. But fortunately it is offset somewhat by the condition of the backhouse, which was torn from its mooring and knocked askew years ago when the pilot of the county snowplow was induced to open the lane. Becoming a bit overinduced, he turned a bit too short and the plow engaged the corner of the backhouse. It has been allowed to remain just as it dropped when Wally Fassett reached over and disengaged the clutch, and the members boast of its generous ventilation and erratic geometry.

Aside from the hearth fire, the sole artificial illumination in the cabin is an old-fashioned kerosene hanging lamp which was salvaged from a country church. Directly beneath it is a table upon which each member, as he enters, deposits his bottle. Additionally, there is a pitcher of the icy spring water that flows perpetually from a pipe in the front yard—water that is agony to the teeth and a frigid benediction to the palate. No one can recall clearly how long the lamp and the table have been there, but all agree that the lamp has leaked kerosene upon the table—and into the water pitcher—ever since it was filched. You may think that the leak might be repaired, or that the table might be moved, or at least that the pitcher might be shifted, but that is because you do not know the Brooklyn Fly Fishers. Every highball that has been consumed in the club during all those years has featured a slight but terribly definite flavor of kerosene

The same willingness to sanctify a traditional disability prevails in the dormitory, the single room constituting the upper floor of the cabin. Here unyielding cots bear mattresses of geologic age, each with its hills and valleys disposed in an individual terrain. Each member has learned how to wind himself between the lumps of his own bed and sleep comfortably in that contorted attitude, and if a newcomer take another member's bed he will hear bitter protestation.

To be at the club for Opening Day is to realize how their devotion to the past inures the members to present hardship. The hardy anglers spend the evening in front of the blast-furnace fireplace, fortifying themselves internally to prevent their entire rear aspects from freezing solid. When the inner stiffness approximates the outer, each picks up a huge load of gray camp blankets and a kerosene lamp and climbs to the loft. How they have failed to burn down the cabin long ago by this procedure is a mystery.

Some take off a few clothes, and there was once an exhibitionist who got into pajamas, but the standard procedure is to take off nothing but the shoes and the hat. Daybreak finds not even an ear or a nose visible, but one cowering figure, more valiant or less enduring than the rest, finally will force himself out of bed to dash downstairs, chunk up the fire, and clench his chattering teeth on the neck of a bottle. When the fire begins to make an impression on the room temperature, the other sleepers come dashing down to seize their bottles and back up to the blaze. The lavatory is the spring-water pipe in the yard. In warm weather they strip down and wash there, shaving with mirrors propped against the porch railing, but on Opening Day they just rinse their hands.

Two things may be noted about that porch in passing. One is that every bottle ever emptied at the club reposes beneath it—it is a broad porch nearly surrounding the cabin, with very little room left under it. The other is that its railing is a favorite spot for the members to cool off in their pelts after a sweaty afternoon in waders—a spectacle that once sent flying two schoolmarms who had driven up the winding lane to inspect the "quaint cabin" thinking it unoccupied.

Two henchmen occupy the club's little world along with the

members. One is Joe Hardenburgh, whose farmhouse lies hidden beyond the apple trees; he "keeps an eye on things" in addition to working a hardscrabble farm on which crops are dragged up painfully rather than raised. This laconic descendant of the patroon who received the far-flung Hardenburgh Patent is best depicted by his reply to an invitation to attend an auction; "You might find something you want," was the inducement. "I got everything I want, now," he said. The other is Bert Cable, the best short-order cook in the world, who looks after the mess hall during the season. He ran the famous White House Restaurant in Roscoe for years and, in fact, starts a restaurant whenever he feels like it, selling out when he gets tired of it. Like Joe, Bert doesn't really work for the club; he just comes up to help out his friends. They are a true part of the atmosphere of this ethereal cosmos.

For so it is. This is the land of the lotus, to enter which is to come under the spell of a dreaming languor, an enchantment of restfulness which makes the world outside hazy and unreal. The energetic visitor ascends the lane in a shower of gravel, hustles in with his equipment, sits down on the porch to catch his breath—and is lost. In this natural bower where nothing can be seen but trees and sky, he idles to watch the line of the hills, to hear the birds at their housekeeping and the river whispering on its stones. He murmurs vague conversation, wanders about the cabin, and dawdles before the fireplace. He smokes the pipe of contemplation over his empty plate. When he goes to his locker for his waders he forgets his purpose; and if he starts for the stream at all he does it late and reluctantly. No one ever strides down to the river at the Brooklyn Fly Fishers. At best, he saunters.

The river itself fits into the spell. This is the Little River, the Beaverkill above its junction with the Willowemoc, the stream to which its alumni return again and again, forsaking the certainties of lordly preserves. The Big River, from the Junction at Roscoe to its junction with the East Branch of the Delaware, is a challenge, whereas the Little River is an invitation. It takes stronger legs and longer chances to wade the Big River, a bigger rod and a better arm to cover its waters. It is here that the ten- and twelve-pound monsters are taken and the five-pound bass that makes the startled angler think he has hooked into a trout twice as big. Here the stalker can watch an hour, a day, or a week until he sees a great trout feeding and then wade armpit-deep and try to keep sixty feet of line off the water as he works out the single cast that will either raise the fish or put him down.

Fishing the Big River is a sport, but fishing the Little River is a recreation. This dozen miles of the loveliest trout water in America, with the Balsam Lake Club at the top and the Brooklyn Fly Fishers at the bottom, is what the old-timers referred to when they wrote about the Beaverkill, the classic water of the Golden Age.

It is still just as it was, at least from the infall of Berry Brook down to the Brooklyn water and the Rockland bridge half a mile below it. A road follows it from Roscoe to the source, but above the Rockland bridge it is a washboarded red-dirt track with an ugly habit of tipping cars into the river, so that visitors to the state campsite above Berry Brook prefer to go in on the paved road from Livingston Manor. All that disturbs the melody of the living countryside along the river road is the bouncing of an occasional farm truck.

And as the river has not changed, neither have the Brooklyn Fly Fishers, for whom the Golden Age still exists. Not for them the state water farther upstream, nor the open water below the Rockland bridge. For years the club leased the beautiful Tempel water in the latter stretch, but they finally gave it up because "nobody ever went down there." No, no one wants to go to any other water. The club leprechaun, Johnny Woodruff, may sneak off to night-fish the Picnic Grounds, and the club juvenile, Ed Myers, may spend his energy on expeditions to the Summer House Pool, but these are the exceptions. Sometimes the members speak knowingly of Foul Rift and the Lone Pine, the Deserted Village, and Painter's Bend, but when you pin them down you discover that they have not fished those pools in the Big River since their boyhood.

Another way remains in which the club stays faithful to the Golden Age. It is the last stand, the loyal Old Guard, the final vanishing remnant of the old-fashioned American dry-fly purists. At first glance it seems strange that this group, more than any other, should exemplify the classic tradition of the dry fly. These are stern and hardy men, unfashionable, contemptuous of innovations, indifferent to foibles; enemies of pretense, averse to strangers, woman-haters; reading no fishing magazines or books—they already know how to fish; immune to British prestige, unknown to Abercrombie's or the Crossroads of Sport, contemptuous of Halford.

But these are the *American* purists. Not for them the long leaders and 4X points, the stream entomology, the tortured science of line calibers and rod action, the elaborate long casting to a rise in still water. Here, as nowhere else, there is exemplified the pure gospel of American dry-fly fishing just as its prophet George LaBranche engraved it on the stone tablets of *The Dry Fly and Fast Water;* as Fred White saw it demonstrated by Theodore Gordon; as Chancellor Levison and Dr. Halsey and all the old-timers who grew up in the great tradition practiced it—the gospel that it doesn't matter what fly you use, it's how and where you use it that counts; the gospel of fishing the water rather than the rise, and covering the broken water rather than the smooth. Every inch of the Brooklyn water is broken, or at least ruffled, at normal tides; every inch of it is fished by the members with the dry fly. And with the dry fly only. Scotty Conover assured the present writer that he had not fished a wet fly in more than thirty years, and he is typical.

Here then is that echo of the Golden Age, that tiny angling Eden that has survived as the Brooklyn Fly Fishers. Would that it were timeless; but its end is early written. Not too many years hence the adjacent waters will be owned by estates instead of individuals, and when they are sold in settlement, the state, that greedy grabber of dead men's water, will surely get them. With state open water at either end of its unguarded stretch of river, hikers swarming over its acres, and cars churning the dust, the club will see its end inevitable. It will sell out to the state, which will dredge the Home Pool for swimming and put a hot-dog stand in the cabin.

The lotus eaters will die of remembrance.

* * *

(Author's note: A number of former and present members of the Brooklyn Fly Fishers have expressed approval of the foregoing article, but they point out that (a) the 1910 calendar was discarded several years ago; (b) the bottles under the porch were sold in a wartime scrap drive; and (c) the lamp has been repaired and no longer leaks kerosene into the water pitcher which, however, still stands on the table beneath it. I record these developments, all of which took place after I wrote the original article, with sadness, for they indicate that change if not progress has at last come to the dreaming land of the lotus.)

THE GOLDEN AGE

GOLDEN TO ME WAS THE DECADE ON THE NEVERSINK THAT
ended with 1940. Edward Ringwood Hewitt had some five
miles of the river between Neversink Village and Hall's Mills,
and his fishing "camp" was an old farmhouse on high ground
overlooking the largest flat along that part of the valley.
Here the "rods" who rented annual fishing privileges used to
assemble at the end of the day for unforgettable nights of
fun and companionship and fishing conversation.

And what a goodly company was there, the choicest spirits
of the angling age, the finest sportsmen, the best fishermen,
the liveliest wits, the best-stored minds; the kindest and most
helpful, too, as we novices quickly learned, and of course
the best of teachers. Here was no stupid competition for big
baskets, no vulgar boasting and lying, none of the boozing
and gambling that are traditional in some camps. These were
the spiritual descendants of Walton, Norris, Hills, Prime,
and Marston, and the atmosphere was the sublimated atmosphere of The Anglers' or The Flyfishers'.

Around, about, and over all was Ed Hewitt, the very monarch of this happy state, discoursing, informing, arguing, teaching, demonstrating—and criticizing. One still remembers his caustic comment—before witnesses, too—that "your fly is all right; the trouble is on the other end of the rod." We always fished our best under his eye and tried to hide our shortcomings from him.

As when, for instance, he took Tom Howell and me to fish in Molly's Pool, one sunset. Ordering us to put on fifteen-foot leaders, he handed us each a No. 16 variant with the most miserably invisible blue hackles imaginable, and clipped off top and bottom, to boot.

"Cast to the edge of the foam," he ordered. "Sparse, you stand here," and he placed me sixty feet below the dam. "Tom, you come over here; I'll show you." Tom was a visitor and it was all new to him.

No honest angler needs to be told that sixty feet is a long way from home plate even with a good rod, which mine was not. I tried and tried but each time fell far short. Apprehending that momentarily my mentor would turn his gaze and his disapproval my way, I wound up with all my strength and threw a mighty backcast and a still mightier forward cast. My line went into the bushes behind me and broke off at the leader knot.

I was undone if he looked my way now, but fortunately I had a leader soaking and another variant. I went frantically to work. I was just finishing my Turle knot when Mr. Hewitt exclaimed:

"What are you doing, Sparse? Don't change that fly!"

"Just tightening the knot, Mr. Hewitt," I replied humbly and not quite mendaciously.

Then my troubles were over, for Tom hooked one of Ed's huge browns. The fish got a move ahead of him and, probably because it was used to being caught and knew all the dodges, headed for a little side stream around the dam below. Then I saw one of the Neversink pictures I shall never forget, the spectacle of Ed Hewitt, seventy years old, running like a deer in his old wading stockings to intercept the fish and at every second step leaping with both feet together to make a splash and scare it back.

It was fun to wade belt-deep, side by side with Mr. Hewitt, up the middle of the glassy Flat Pool casting (he right-handed and I left-handed) to the fish that lay along either bank under the alders. It was a far shot on water that excused no errors, and it took more eyesight than I had even then to see the little sipping rise with which a four-pound brown would take a tiny wet fly or a thinly tied variant. Ed got all the fish, as I recall, but I got most of the fun.

It was even more fun to pursue the variation of night fishing that Mr. Hewitt developed for his water, which was improved with numerous low, sloping dams having deep undercuts beneath them in which any number of big fish harbored during the daylight hours. As the light failed, they would come out and begin feeding under the foam where the water came over the dam, and then for a brief period one who was a good angler could have rare sport fishing a close-clipped variant to the edge of the foam.

When it became dark, the big fish would drop down still farther and feed below the foam, and then we would use a No. 13 Hewitt wet stonefly on the same fifteen-foot 4X gut leader. This was cast up and across, and as it came down, the rod point was raised and slack drawn in so that the fly was kept jogging along without drag—not an easy thing to do by guesswork in total darkness.

The fish did not hit hard but sucked in the fly, and it was largely by sixth sense and divination that one had to judge when to tighten. Then, if the angler were fortunate, he would feel a gentle pluck quickly building up to a powerful pull. The succeeding action was always violent and almost always brief, for these were strong, heavy fish. There would be a tremendous splash and a hard vibration of the rod tip, another heavy splash simultaneous with a hard jerk, all within a space of two seconds, and then the angler would reel in and put on a new fly. With the exception of Mr. Hewitt, we seldom landed those fish.

But the thrill still lingers in my memory. I love to recall the July evenings I used to spend standing knee-deep on a smooth, sandy bottom that dived abruptly down to six feet close below the dam, watching the starry sky and the white, white lace of foam where the water fell, hearing the night sounds in the black woods towering over me on the steep far bank, tasting the mellowness of Kentucky burley in my pipe, and still concentrating every taut faculty on taking up slack at the right speed.

Particularly do I treasure the memory of such an evening, the last time Ed Hewitt and I night-fished together. It was just sunset when we drove down to the Meadow Pool in his ancient Buick touring car with the top aluminum-painted to reflect the heat and holes cut in the back curtain through which to shove rods. In front of us was the great wide dam of the Meadow Pool, the blue water of its undercut covered with a tracery of white foam, with room on the brilliant white sand below for four or five to fish abreast.

From a distance which was daunting to me but merely respectful to Mr. Hewitt we cast invisible blue variants, clipped so they floated in rather than on the surface, for an hour or more, he with his usual success and I with mine. Although he cast with an ungraceful chopping motion, the result of an old shoulder injury, and seemed to sock the iron into his fish like a Nantucket harpooner, there was nothing wrong with the way Mr. Hewitt's line went out to its target; and as long as I knew him, I never knew him to break a leader. So while he caught fish, I watched, mostly; that way, each of us was getting what he best enjoyed.

A rain squall came suddenly over the mountain and hammered at us. I glanced at my companion, but he continued to ply his rod and paid no attention to the downpour that quickly soaked us. He was in his seventies at the time, and I decided that if he could stand it, I could.

The rain was tapering off when Ed remarked, "Hello, it's raining; let's get in the car." He stumbled as he waded out of the pool, but as he quickly recovered and paid no attention, I thought nothing of it. By the time we had stowed the rods, the shower had stopped and darkness had fallen.

"Let's go up in the tail of the Camp Pool," Ed suggested and drove the hundred yards or so that we had to go.

We started fishing with our same fine leaders and the little No. 13 stoneflies. Usually that was the best bet on that water, but tonight the fish would not take, although we knew they must be there and feeding. When I next heard from Mr. Hewitt, he was halfway up the pool.

"Hey, Sparse, they want something big. Put on a heavy leader and a salmon fly."

He had changed fly and leader in the dark and had been

experimenting. I followed suit and was still fumbling when I heard a heavy splash and a savage exclamation from my companion. "Ha! Got him!" he cried with as much exultation as if he had not hooked a fish all summer. The fact was that fishing was to Mr. Hewitt what whisky is to a drunkard; he couldn't get along without it. Four or five times during the course of every day you would see him drop his work, hastily slip on his old wading stockings, and go down to the river with his rod. In a few minutes he would be playing a fish, and in a few minutes more he would be back at work.

And yet, that night, he experienced as much wild elation over hooking a big fish—a fish which he tossed back carelessly after playing it in—as I would have who, naturally, never caught anything.

It was near midnight when Ed finally called quits and we went back to the camp, where he and I happened to be the only occupants at the time. As we sat on the porch steps and took off our wading gear, I was astounded to see him coolly dump a quart of water out of each of his wading stockings. He had filled them when he stumbled at the dam, thus completing the soaking that the shower had begun. But quit while there was fishing to be done? Not Ed Hewitt!

We changed to dry clothes, and then he made a pot of tea for himself and for me broke out a bottle of Edradour, a fabulous pot-still Scotch twenty-five years old that no words of mine can describe. We ate a sandwich and then went into the common room, where my friend made a couch out of pillows on the window seat.

"Sparse," he said when he had arranged it to suit him, "you've been after me for a long time to write my reminiscences, and I've finally made a start. Listen to this."

And then, while I smoked a pipe and sipped my whisky, he read me the bright narrative which became one of the best chapters in his fascinating autobiography, *Those Were the Days*. I can hear his voice yet and see the tackle-littered common room in the lamplight, and I cherish this memory, for the camp is gone now and all that lovely stretch of river where we fished is underneath Neversink Reservoir in sixty feet of water, and Ed long ago crossed that other River to fish from the far bank. That evening was a fragment of the Golden Age, both of the Neversink and of me.

WORDS AT PARTING

(The concluding paragraph of *Days and Nights of Salmon Fishing* by William Scrope. Suggested by Franklin H. Smith of The Anglers' Club of New York.)

"FAREWELL THEN, DEAR BROTHERS OF THE ANGLE; AND when you go forth to take your pleasure, either in the mountain stream that struggles and roars through the narrow pass, or in the majestic salmon river that sweeps in lucid mazes through the vale, may your sport be ample and your hearts light! But should the fish prove more sagacious than yourself—a circumstance, excuse me, that is by no means impossible—should they, alas (but fate avert it), reject your hookèd gifts, the course of the river will always lead you to pleasant places. In these we leave you to the quiet enjoyment of the glorious works of the Creation, whether it be your pleasure to go forth when the Spring sheds its flowery fragrance, or in the more advanced season when the sere leaf is shed incessantly and wafted on the surface of the swollen river."